Not in the Public Interest

by

Patti Allen-Price

&

Bryon Williams

Based on a true story

Copyright © Patti Allen-Price & Bryon Williams 2018

Other books by Bryon Williams:

A Light at the End (memoir)

Code Name Millicent (Comedy/crime)

The Tourist from the Light (Paranormal)

The Reluctant Psychic (Paranormal)

Naked Warrior (Paranormal Erotica)

The Psychic Spy (Paranormal)

The Twilight Escort Agency (Comedy)

The Burning Boy (Action Adventure)

Dedicated to our darling daughter

Tracyanne

Our love always

Patti and Dennis

Disclaimer

Although most of the events that follow are based on a true story and are as accurate as can be ascertained from information in the public domain, some are the product of supposition and fictional interpretation and it is up to the reader to decide which are which. The names, apart from the co-writer, have been changed to protect the innocent unwittingly caught up in this tragedy and to prevent the guilty from receiving any more undeserved notoriety. May their names be forever lost in the mists of time and fading memories.

Apart from the co-writer, Patti Allen-Price, any similarity between the names mentioned and any actual person is purely coincidental and fictional and do not refer to any person living.

Prologue

Patti was in the kitchen watching the news on television as she prepared breakfast. Dennis, her husband, who had been in the living room tinkling away at the piano, composing yet another song, wandered into the kitchen.

'Another hit on the way,' he said with a wry grin. 'You don't appreciate what a brilliant, talented husband you have.'

'Of course I do,' Patti replied absently, her eyes glued to the screen. 'Just don't expect me to keep complimenting you all the time.'

She waved her hand, gesturing him to keep quiet and pointed at the screen. 'There's been a terrible murder on the Gold Coast – a young woman. Bashed and strangled. She was found near a golf course. Apparently she was killed last night. A security officer found her this morning. How terrible.'

They watched as paramedics carried the covered body on a stretcher towards a waiting ambulance parked among the police cars. A small uncovered foot poked out from beneath the cover. A few morbidly interested witnesses stood behind a barrier, gawking at the macabre sight.

'Oh, Dennis, what a terrible tragedy. Just think what the poor girl's family must be going through.'

'They probably don't know yet,' Dennis replied. 'It'll be a bit soon. She'll have to be identified first.'

'Just think how we'd be feeling if that was Tianne.' Patti shuddered at the thought.

'Any chance of breakfast?' Dennis asked dismissing the news item and turning to leave the room.

'You blind?' Patti called as he left. 'Cereal, toast and coffee on the table,' she said pointing at the meal on the table, 'waiting for you to finish your symphony. I've had mine.'

Three days later two policemen arrived at the front door.

'Mrs Price?'

Patti nodded uncertainly.

'Can we come in? I'm afraid we have some bad news for you.'

Patti felt increasingly uneasy as she led them through to the kitchen.

'You have a daughter by the name of Tianne?'

Patti nodded again, her heartbeat beginning to rise in alarm.

Chapter 1

Patti sat on the balcony of their luxury apartment in a green striped deck chair overlooking the busy marina on Paphos harbour and the glorious, aqua-blue Mediterranean Sea. She wore a pair of figure-hugging white shorts which accentuated her bronzed dancer's legs and a yellow sleeveless blouse caught up and tied in a knot under her shapely bosom, leaving her already tanned and flat midriff bare to the Limassol sun. Cyprus was absolute heaven compared to cold and blustery England where they'd recently lived and worked. She and Dennis had been booked for a three-month season at La Boite, a popular restaurant and night spot, and in a short time had become known in and around Limassol as 'The English Entertainers', which irked Patti as she was fiercely Irish.

Dennis's lean, lanky body appeared in the doorway. 'Happy with the rehearsal this morning?' he asked.

'Yes,' Patti replied. 'The new numbers worked well, I thought. Your arrangements are wonderful as usual and the harmonies are great.'

'Let's face it, Batman, we make a dynamic duo,' Dennis grinned.

'And modest,' Patti smiled. 'I think I might wear that new aqua silk dress with the beads and sequins tonight, what do you think?'

Looking out to translucent sea, Dennis replied, 'Sort of match the shimmering water out there, yes?'

Patti nodded. 'I wonder if the tourists will get the connection.'

'If they're not too pissed,' he smirked. 'What time does Tianne arrive?'

'Late this afternoon. Should be well in time for the show tonight. It will be wonderful to see her again. She'll be pleased to be out of London for a while.'

Dennis nodded. 'Do you know her plans?' he asked.

'You know Tianne, always on the go. I think she'll hang around Cyprus for a while before heading back. Give her time to thaw out and recuperate before hitting the drama teaching and audition slog.'

Apart from being a loving husband with a wry sense of humour, Dennis was a brilliant musician, arranger, composer and accompanist for Patti's act. He was born in Birmingham in the United Kingdom and started his career on stage as one of Tommy Steele's Steelmen. He also appeared in the film, *The Tommy Steele Story*, and was manager for Tommy for three years.

As well as working as Patti's accompanist and co-arranger, he had a fine voice and sang harmony in the act with Patti. He had also performed with the Polka Dots, the UK's top vocal group, for eight years and they appeared regularly on the BBC's *Sunday Night at the Palladium* and at several Royal Command performances. He also worked with many American greats including Bob Hope, Peggy Lee and Ella Fitzgerald whom he adored so he was no slouch in show business.

Dennis and Patti worked excellently together as a duo and were very popular in England, Cyprus and Australia. This was the second marriage for both and he became stepfather to Tianne.

Tianne did arrive on time and went straight to the restaurant where she dined on the terrace alone before the show started. She was an independent, impetuous, gregarious, beautiful 25-year old brunette, often likened to Elizabeth Taylor, but with amazing large green eyes that betrayed a knowledge of life far beyond her years. She walked with grace and her slim figure made her appear taller than she actually was.

She greeted her mother and stepfather effusively in the dressing room shortly after their first show.

'Great show,' she beamed as they group hugged. 'Love the new numbers and you look amazing, Mum, like you just washed in on the tide.'

Dennis turned to Patti. 'See, someone got the connection.'

'Not sure it's a compliment,' Patti laughed. 'I sound like a bit of old water-logged driftwood.'

Tianne became a regular at the club and with her outgoing nature and connection with the popular English entertainers soon became accepted by the young smart set that frequented the venue. Because of its mild weather, glorious beaches, luxurious accommodation, natural beauty and proximity to Greece, Turkey, Russia, the Middle East, Europe and Africa, Limassol was an exciting hotbed of intrigue and mystery with shady characters of organised crime, the drug trade, finance and business and intelligence agencies from around the world congregating to buy, sell and trade their wares, mostly in secrecy. As a result, Limassol was one of the safest cities in the world with an enviable low local crime rate, it not being wise to shit in your own backyard. It was another Casablanca and Humphrey Bogart and Ingrid Bergman would have been quite at home there.

The Insignificant Man sat alone in the back of La Boite's bar and entertainment room sipping a Scotch and soda, his inscrutable dark brown eyes casually straying around the assembled customers, the backgrounds of most of whom he was only too aware. He had a perfect view of the room and the adjoining patio where patrons relaxed in the cool evening air. He constantly noted who was dining with whom and who was in deep, secretive conversation with associates.

He was an Australian of mixed Middle Eastern parentage, in his early forties, of average height, with an ordinary slim face of unremarkable features and unreadable expression, dark straight hair cut short and tanned skin stretched over a slim but deceptively strong body honed by regular exercise. He wore a smart but nondescript two-button grey suit, white shirt and light blue tie secured by a plain gold pin, grey socks and black lace-up shoes and, one would imagine, white Jockey Y-front shorts.

Tonight he was going by the name of Max, one of the many aliases he used depending on the company he was keeping and the role he was playing at any particular time. He had been particularly interested when the beautiful, extrovert Tianne arrived on the scene a few days earlier and had soon discovered her name, nationality, her occupation as an actress, her background and relationship with Patti and Dennis.

He watched her speculatively for some time as she laughed and danced with a young American boy who had arrived with a gorgeous German heiress whose billionaire father was in the oil business. He then gestured to another young man who was obviously in the same party and the young man smiled, excused himself and made his way over to The Insignificant Man's table. The young man bent and listened to Max's whispered instructions for a few minutes, nodded and moved back to his friends, leading Tianne off the dance floor and back to their table where he entered into a light-hearted conversation with her about places she must see while she was in Cyprus.

The next day, at the young man's suggestion, Tianne hired a car and took off to explore the beautiful coast up to the ancient port of Larnaca. Although she'd only recently arrived on Cyprus she was eager to experience as much as she could. Patti and Dennis waved her off with no suspicion that this day would set in motion events that would change all of their lives forever.

Chapter 2

Patti was always going to be a performer. She was born in the incredibly beautiful county of Wicklow in south-east Ireland and always considered herself Irish. She would always remember the happy times in that idyllic county of vivid green and playing on Silver Strand beach which was often deserted and perfect for an escape from grown-ups. As a child she was subconsciously steeped in the Irish Roman Catholic church and Celtic mythology. It was on Silver Strand beach at the age of three that Patti had what she later considered her first psychic experience. As a small child she had no concept of psychic phenomena and accepted it as perfectly normal but the vivid memory remained with her for life.

She was walking alone on the beach and suddenly became aware of a young man with short blond hair and dressed in a RAF uniform walking beside her. It was 1944 and the war raged in Europe. He was very handsome with the kindest blue eyes she'd ever seen and she did not in any way feel threatened. He asked if he could walk with her for a while. He took her hand and they talked. He told her many things of her life to come. She told him how scared she was of the war and he replied she would be perfectly safe, the war would soon be over and she was not to worry as everything was going to turn out well. He pointed to something out to sea and Patti turned to look and when she turned back the young man was gone and the beach was deserted. She looked back down the beach wondering where her new friend had gone and noticed there was only one set of footprints on the sand: hers.

Shortly after that, she and her family moved to up-market Bassett Green in Southampton in England when she was almost four years old. Her father became an ordinance surveyor, joining his father who was Borough Surveyor for Hastings, and after an excellent education, her father had moved on to Sandhurst and became an officer in the Army during the Second World War. Her parents separated a few years after the war and her mother gained sole custody of Patti and her two brothers: Brian, the elder, and Kieran, the younger. She was never told why her parents separated as they were only children and it wasn't considered necessary in those days. Children were to be seen and preferably not heard and they must never betray their emotions in public. It just wasn't done in polite society. Conservative good manners were drilled into her and she must always behave like an upper-class young lady as befitted her upbringing.

In her teenage years Patti was awarded a scholarship at St Anne's Convent Grammar school where she studied ballet, classical singing, dramatic art and piano with passion, which set the pattern for the rest of her life.

To the shock and horror of her dance tutor, Patti's mother decided to follow her eldest son, Brian, to Australia in 1957.

'Orstralia?' Miss Benton had intoned in revulsion. 'Good heavens, why? An uncultured race of ex-convicts on the other side of the world who play dreadful rough sports and drink beer,' she sneered. 'And they don't even have a national ballet or opera company. What about your career in the theatre, child?'

But Patti's mother, still relatively young in her forties, was determined to make a fresh start in a new country so she bundled Kieran and Patti onto the next available ship and sailed for Sydney.

Although only at the age at fifteen, Patti followed her dream and continued studying and searched for theatre work in culturally backward Australia. Eventually she was asked to audition in Sydney as a replacement for a famous vaudeville star who was leaving the cast of a show at the Theatre Royal in Brisbane. Being classically trained, Patti had never even heard of vaudeville but it was the only work on offer. She auditioned for the producer and was successful so instead of a pirouette and *ballet blanc* in a white tutu she learned to sing and bump and grind in sequins and high heels. But under her mother's strict instructions, she avoided the nude scenes as nudes weren't quite respectable and were not allowed to move on stage. Also the nudes were artfully draped and posed at the back of the stage and Patti always worked front of stage, so she actually avoided even seeing the nudes during the performance, which her mother approved of.

It was at the Theatre Royal that she met her soon-to-be close friend and fellow singing featured artist, Maggie, who was approximately the same age, and the friendship and mutual support continued for the rest of their lives.

Patti never really enjoyed vaudeville and after three months decided to leave. She had often sat alone on the stage after the performance when everybody else had left and dreamed of appearing in what she considered 'legitimate' theatre. But one night she left the theatre, having decided to hand in her notice, and stood at the entrance of the cobbled lane that led from the stage door to the street, feeling despondent. It was a dark winter's night and a fog lay over the city giving it a mysterious atmosphere. Suddenly an elderly man appeared out of the wispy fog and walked up to her. She was at first a little apprehensive but the elderly man seemed harmless and non-threatening. He stopped in front of her and smiled.

'Keep going,' he said, 'you're going to make it.'

It was almost as if he was reading her mind and she was quite puzzled but with another reassuring smile he walked on into the fog and disappeared. She decided it was a sign from heaven and at that moment decided not to resign after all.

After a couple of years Patti moved into the newly developed live television industry with a contract with HSV Channel 7 as one of the featured artists in the top-rating, live-to-air vaudeville shows, *Theatre Royal* and *Club Seven*, starring the popular comedian, George Wallace Jr. He always looked after her and supported her in her career.

Her voice, looks and dancing skills brought her to the attention of the producers and before long she was performing solo along with magicians, jugglers, tumblers, adagio and other speciality acts. She was soon in demand all over Australia, which led to nightclub work and Australia-wide attention.

Patti met a handsome, young, up-and-coming businessman, Mike, and fell in love but her drive and dreams of performing never left her. Their marriage in their late teens was predictably disastrous despite the birth of their daughter, Tianne, and they separated and divorced five years later. There was other music to dance to, other roles to play. But Tianne was the most important and loved person in her life and Patti had no intention of losing her daughter. She was awarded custody but allowing for her biological father's love and not wanting to disturb her education, she came to an agreement with Mike that he would have care of her during school terms at St Rita's and Patti would keep in constant contact between engagements and assume full care during holidays.

Later, in Melbourne, where she was performing and representing Queensland in a Hector Crawford produced television talent show, *Showcase*, for GTV Channel Nine, she became friendly with the handsome English musical director, Dennis Price, and they soon became close friends and eventually lovers. Unbeknown to Patti, Dennis was married and when she found out, broke off the relationship despite still being in love with the attractive musician. He assured her he was getting a divorce but Patti was determined not to be the reason for another marriage break-up. The affair was over. Hurt and in despair, she accepted a contract to entertain the troops in Vietnam during the disastrous war there and was a hit with the troops who were eager for entertainment and the sight of beautiful Australian female entertainers.

On her return from Saigon, she travelled back to Melbourne for work and unexpectedly Dennis contacted her again, telling her he was now divorced and a free man and wanted desperately to re-establish their former relationship. Patti, still attracted but wary, insisted on marriage and Dennis proposed. With Tianne acting as bridesmaid, they married in Melbourne and continued working together as musical director-accompanist and vocalist. On the day of the wedding, Tianne called her father on the Gold Coast and told him she had decided to stay with her mother and Dennis and would not be returning to live in Queensland with him and his new wife who seemed to resent Tianne. They continued to live in Melbourne until Dennis was offered a great opportunity to work as the musical director of the new 'Top of the State' venue in Brisbane.

Patti, Dennis and Tianne moved back to Brisbane and rented a house in the suburbs and Tianne continued with her schooling at St Rita's convent. Like her mother she had a strong desire to perform and studied Music and Drama and their relationship flourished.

Tianne grew into a beautiful, talented young woman but became wilful, determined and very independent in her teenage years. Like many young women, she became quite a handful to manage, skipping school and sneaking out at night down a long ladder she'd placed outside her bedroom window unbeknown to Patti and Dennis. When Patti discovered the ladder she took it down and hid it away and when Tianne returned home at 3.00am from a 'rave', she was unable to get back inside until well after sunrise. But it didn't cure her of her rebellious nature. At seventeen, Tianne eventually moved out of home and shared an apartment and freedom from parental control with one of her friends, unknowingly sowing the seeds for the disaster that was to follow.

Dennis and Patti received word from Dennis's family in England that his mother had contracted cancer and was not expected to survive so they decided to move to England to care for her during this trying time. They left for England, joined Actors Equity and settled in Blackpool where they soon picked up duo work in Birmingham, Coventry, Newquay, the Channel Islands, South Wales and all over the UK.

While staying in theatrical digs in Troy-de-rue in Wales, Patti was hanging out some washing on the clothes line when a movement caught her attention. The back garden overlooked a small hill and Patti could see a man's figure slowly appearing up over the hill. The man was dressed as an Arab in caftan and *keffiyeh*. For some strange reason Patti's heart started to pound as the man slowly approached and suddenly everything blacked out and she fainted. Other members of the household came running as they heard her muffled scream as she fell. They revived her then laughed as they told her one of the men had dressed up as an Arab to surprise her and they didn't expect it to have such a potent effect on her. Patti also couldn't understand why the sight of an Arab would cause her to faint as Middle Eastern men had never been frightening to her but it obviously had shocked her enough to cause her to black out. Was it a portent of things to come?

Patti auditioned for a revival of *South Pacific* and out of hundreds of other hopefuls who auditioned across the UK, won the role of Bloody Mary. The show opened in the Belgrade Theatre in Coventry to moderate reviews but disappointingly did not transfer to London's West End as was expected. However, Patti won rave reviews for her role, which enhanced her image further and cemented her position as a local 'star'.

Unexpectedly, Dennis's mother's condition improved as she responded to treatment and she went on to survive for another seven years by which time Patti and Dennis had become very popular performers and in fairly constant work.

An opportunity came to audition for a three-month season at a venue in Cyprus, La Boite, in Limassol, an internationally popular tourist resort, and needing a break away from England's dismal weather, they accepted. They impressed at the audition and were offered the contract. Three months turned into twelve and Patti and Dennis were delighted to remain, forever if possible, living in the luxury of a beautiful, spacious, marble-floored apartment with a huge terrace, overlooking the incredibly beautiful Mediterranean Sea and the busy marina. They were within a short walking distance to their place of work with the added bonus of the La Boite swimming pool which they were free to use. Loving the Cyprus life so much, Patti invited Tianne over for a holiday, completely forgetting that a year before they left England Tianne had told her that she'd been to a clairvoyant who told her if she ever went near the Middle East she would suffer a stab in the heart. Although many psychic predictions do not come true, that was one prediction she should have taken notice of.

Chapter 3

Tianne drove up the coast to the thriving port of Larnaca, the third largest city on Cyprus, established in the thirteenth century, with the remains of Phoenician temples and the ancient sea port and its palm-lined seafront, and marvelled at the beautiful scenery along the coast. She booked into the Pasithea youth hostel and immediately began exploring the area. The air-conditioned hostel was only ten minutes' walk from the beach, five minutes from Mackenzie Beach and its amazing outdoor cafes, and a fifteen-minute walk from the town centre and Finikoudes Beach. It was a perfect location.

That night she went to the trendy Fish Bowl nightclub and bar that the young guy in Limassol had recommended. The music was loud, the lighting hypnotic, and the place was packed and raging. Tianne walked in and was immediately greeted by people she'd never seen before. A bit different from the rather staid and 'respectable, La Boite, she thought. She ordered a vodka cocktail at the bar and stood watching the spectacle of young shirtless men standing on the bar mixing drinks for the waiting crowd while the music pumped out and everybody was dancing.

Presently an extremely attractive young man approached her and they began talking, which wasn't all that easy with the noise level of the music. He introduced himself as Rashid and asked her about herself. She told him she was an actress from Australia and he was suitably astonished.

'I too am an actor,' he said, obviously surprised and smiling broadly, showing perfect white teeth, which knocked Tianne for a six. 'I did a lot of work in Cairo, TV and stage, and I also have done many commercials. I also played the lead in a *Tarzan* series on television,' he said modestly.

Well, you've certainly got the body and looks for it, she thought, appraising his body speculatively when he turned his head away.

'I'm an Australian but I've been working and studying in London,' she said. 'My parents are entertainers too. They're working in Limassol at the La Boite and I've just joined them for a holiday.'

'They're not the English Entertainers I've heard about, are they?' he asked.

'Yes, they are,' she laughed. 'Don't tell me you've heard of them.'

'Of course, they are quite famous here on Cyprus,' he said, obviously impressed.

'Well, I might take you up there and introduce you sometime if you like,' she laughed.

'That is a date,' he said. 'I love show people.'

'Oh, they're show people all right,' she grinned.

They danced and talked for the rest of the night, enjoying each other's company enormously. He walked her home at 4.00am and declined her invitation to come inside for coffee.

'I would like to see you again, though, if that is possible,' he said in a gentlemanly way. 'Tomorrow if you are available?'

'That'd be wonderful,' she replied.

Chapter 4

Patti didn't hear from Tianne for several days. She was lying by the pool where they spent many happy hours bathing in the glorious sun and mixing with the many international tourists who frequented Cyprus and the La Boite venue, when Tianne suddenly appeared, accompanied by one of the most beautiful men that Patti had ever seen. Both were in swimming costume and made an eye-catching couple as they made their way across the terrace to Patti. Tianne lightly kissed her mother on the cheek, which was surprising as neither of the women were demonstrative of their feelings. She smiled and introduced the young man as Rashid.

'I've been staying at a hostel in Larnaca. We've just been diving on the Zenobia wreck,' she said. 'A hundred and four articulated fully loaded lorries that sank in 1980! It was so beautiful. And earlier Rashid took me to see Aphrodite's rock,' she said excitedly as she put her hand on his arm. 'I also went to Lania Village and had a look at the beautiful Virgin Mary of Asinou Church. Amazing.

Rashid didn't come into the church of course; he's Muslim.'

Rashid was in his mid-twenties, of average height, beautifully muscled with a perfect Mediterranean olive complexion, white even teeth, dark, short, curly hair and playful dark, almost black, eyes that gave him the appearance of a cheeky, vulnerable youth. His English was halting and accented but excellent, which only added to his charm and appeal. Patti was mesmerised.

After a few minutes of small chat, Rashid excused himself and went to the bar for cold drinks as women's and a few men's eyes followed him all the way. Tianne revealed he was originally from Tehran and she had met him at the trendy Fish Bowl nightclub in Larnaca, further up the coast, which he presently managed while he was 'resting'. She said he was really an actor, trained in the Agouza Community United Academy of Dramatic Art and had majored in Performing Arts Theatre/Acting at the A.I.A.E University in Cairo where his parents were living at the time. He had appeared in many television commercials, series and films throughout the Middle East. It was obvious that Tianne was smitten with this Iranian god-like young man and casually mentioned he was married with two small children living in Cairo.

Despite her liking the young man, a small chill passed down Patti's spine and she hoped Tianne wouldn't get hurt as it was obvious they were an item. Tianne assured her they were 'just good friends', but Patti with her own life experiences still felt dubious about the relationship.

Rashid returned with their drinks and they chatted amicably for a few minutes until Tianne excused herself to visit the ladies' room. It was then Rashid told Patti that he was very attracted to Tianne and asked if she would mind if they stayed together with Patti and Dennis in their apartment for a few days before returning to Larnaca.

Alarm bells immediately rang in Patti's head. 'But Tianne said you're married with a couple of small children,' she said.

It was then Rashid said something that would stay in Patti's mind forever. He shook his head almost sadly and said, 'They live in Cairo. We have been apart so long that I have forgotten all about them. It is like they no longer exist.'

Patti was astonished and horrified that he could talk this way about his wife and two small children. If he could treat them like this, what hurt could he bring to her daughter?

'I'm sorry,' Patti said firmly. 'I'm broadminded but, no, that and any relationship would be totally unacceptable.'

Rashid's expression went completely blank as he stared into Patti's eyes for a long time.

'I understand,' he said.

Tianne returned and Rashid immediately rose and took her by the arm. 'We must be returning to Larnaca, Tianne, I have business to attend to,' he said.

'But…' a bemused Tianne said as he guided her toward the exit. 'Mum…?'

'Call me,' Patti called after them as they disappeared.

Patti rose from her Li-lo and hurried to the low stone wall that separated the pool area from the street and looked over. A group of noisy young men were gathered around nearby parked cars. Rashid gestured to them and urged Tianne into the passenger side of her hire car, got in the driver's seat and drove off. The other cars followed.

Chapter 5

Rashid

Wearing jeans, shirt and flak jacket, Rashid sat amongst the ruins of a former upmarket menswear store in war-ravaged West Beirut. The detritus of fashionable clothing lay scattered and destroyed amongst the dirt, broken concrete and glass. The stock of his Egyptian version of the Swedish Carl Gustav M45, dubbed the 'Port Said', sub-machine gun pressed into his shoulder, his eye lined up on the sights. From his hidden position he was unnoticeable. At any minute now the heads of the government militia fighter patrol would cautiously appear over the remains of the frame of the smashed front window leaving them exposed to his line of fire. Rashid waited patiently.

As he expected the heads of three uniformed government men slowly rose simultaneously into his view. He gently squeezed the trigger and a deadly hail of M45 lead spewed into the unsuspecting victims, cutting them to pieces. He waited, prepared for some form of retaliation, but none was forthcoming. They must've been a small patrol, he thought. For Beirut in 1981 it was relatively quiet apart from the distant sounds of war despite yet another current ceasefire. A sudden burst of machine gun fire was not unusual. He noticed a rather smart and relatively undamaged red and white check scarf hanging from a splintered wooden shelf just above his head. Pulling it down he tied it around his head in the form of a bandana. A smashed mirror nearby was sufficient to show his reflection and he smiled in satisfaction at the effect. He looked exactly the part of a dashing freedom fighter.

Rashid had been radicalised into the PLO at Cairo University where he was ostensibly studying drama and television techniques. His doting successful middle-class family had originally attempted to inveigle him into a business degree but Rashid had dreams of stardom, fame and fortune and as always his parents succumbed to his pleading. He and a couple of Palestinian classmates, Abdi and Farid, who were also hopeful actors and film stars, had attended a lecture at a coffee shop where Yasser Arafat was speaking to a crowd of students regaling the virtues of the PLO and its struggles against the invading Israeli army who were determined to wipe out any Palestinian home rule. Arafat was charismatic and convincing, insisting that armed rebellion and terrorism were the only ways to defeat the usurpers of their rightful homeland. He said, 'Our basic aim is to liberate the land from the Mediterranean Sea to the Jordan River. We are not concerned with what took place in June 1967 or in eliminating the consequences of the June War. The Palestinian revolution's basic concern is the uprooting of the Zionist entity from our land and liberating it.'

This impressed Rashid and many other idealistic young people around the world who flocked to his cause.

Arafat's rhetoric and logic regarding the struggle of the poor against the rich, the wealthy right against the socialist left, appealed to the romantic, adventurous young men in search of action and adventure and soon they became radicalised and members of the PLO and the Al Fatah. However, the war in Lebanon was not a religious war; this was a war of the privileged ruling class, the leftover influence of the rich French colonialists against the thousands of underprivileged Palestinians who, as despised refugees, were forced to flee their homeland by the formation of the Jewish State of Israel.

Rashid had become a fanatical follower and even had 'Member of the PLO' written across the top of his birth certificate. He and his two friends had been sent to southern Lebanon for three months' training where they eagerly learnt the art of killing before being recruited into action. Abdi and Farid had been killed in the first month of fighting but Rashid remained unscathed. His first kill had been a wealthy accountant government fighter who had mistakenly fallen prey to the beautiful young man with the lean, strong body and bewitching smile at one of the constant political demonstrations. Rashid encouraged his advances until he was led through the back alleyways past devastated buildings, burnt-out tanks and bomb craters to a deserted building that had once been a block of apartments. The accountant made a sexual advance on him and Rashid responded until he was in the arms of the plump, sexually aroused, middle-aged man. He then laughed and slipping a knife from his waistband sash, suddenly stabbed his would-be suitor several times in the stomach and chest. The man's eyes opened wide in shock at the unexpected attack and slowly slid down Rashid's body to the floor where, bleeding profusely, he died at Rashid's feet.

Rashid found the killing exhilarating and the adrenaline pumped through his body. After that, killing became a passion and the opportunities became almost endless in that frenzied theatre of war.

There were so many factions involved it was sometimes difficult to tell friend from foe. But as the months of chaos continued and the political climate and leaders seemed to change constantly the PLO began to lose influence. Israeli forces entered the country after an assassination attempt on their ambassador in London by Palestinian dissidents had failed. They mounted a huge attack from the south of Lebanon and pushed north with superior weapons and manpower. Their original aim was to wipe out Palestinian guerrilla bases near the Israeli border but their forces pushed further north destroying any opposition along the way. They eventually entered Beirut and by force of superior numbers and political opposition and in-fighting, Arafat was forced to relinquish his position and retreat to Tunisia where he made his headquarters just outside Tunis. Arafat's departure from Lebanon was an agreed evacuation of the PLO from Beirut and thousands of Palestinians who remained cheered their leader as he left the PLO offices at the port. Large areas of the once beautiful and prosperous city had been reduced to rubble after seven years of conflict mostly sparked by Arafat's presence. His departure was a terrible blow to Palestinian hopes of regaining their former homeland.

Most of the PLO fighters dispersed to Cyprus and some to Jordan, Syria, Iraq, Sudan and north and south Yemen. Some went to Greece but as the new headquarters were set up in Tunisia, Rashid followed the big guns of the PLO to gain influence. But the slide continued and Rashid found himself becoming disillusioned with Arafat's stance of negotiation instead of war and terrorism and transferred to Cyprus where many Palestinians from Lebanon had fled.

It was there that Rashid met The Insignificant Man who turned out to be an agent for a clandestine

Australian intelligence organisation. Hearing Rashid had become disenchanted with Yasser Arafat's new stand on terrorism The Insignificant Man set about turning him into a double agent to get information on PLO activity and any involvement in Australia. Rashid turned but was very careful with the information he provided, passing on only just enough to satisfy his new handler, but he would always ostensibly remain a PLO agent.

There was little acting work in Cyprus so he flew to Cairo to advance his career and continue his undercover work as an agent for the PLO. Mainly because of his looks, which had matured, and his natural charm he soon began getting work in television and the occasional film which appeared all over the Middle East, and although he kept in touch with the PLO his ego demanded more.

But the PLO weren't to be toyed with and they demanded he fulfil his obligations. He was moved around as an agent in Egypt and various countries where his diverse 'talents' were required. He was very active in Algiers during the conflict there and a newspaper photographer caught a picture of him receiving a payment of a large sum of money from a known PLO operative in London.

He was eventually moved back to Cyprus for undercover work and being an actor he was, of course, well equipped to play the role of a waiter and was soon offered a job at a trendy nightclub, the Fish Bowl, in Larnaca. There he met a beautiful Egyptian Muslim girl, Nareen, who was also a PLO sympathiser and freedom fighter and they married a few months later. His parents weren't invited to the wedding as they had become estranged while he fought in Lebanon. Within two years he had fathered two young sons and they lived in an apartment in Larnaca. This did not interrupt Rashid's social life at all and he was soon carousing with international tourists and jet-setters who frequented the club. Nareen, being a good Muslim wife, was relegated to the home and caring for the family.

As prearranged through The Insignificant Man, Rashid met the beautiful and flirtatious Australian girl, the daughter of the English Entertainers he'd heard about who were appearing in Limassol. Not only was she beautiful, he'd learned she was also an actress and they followed a common goal. He desperately needed a passport to either America or Australia to continue his PLO assignment to set up a Young Palestinian Movement in either country and set about seducing her in order to travel on her passport. Despite his association with an Australian intelligence organisation he was unable to obtain an Australian passport because of his PLO affiliations. Tianne was a willing partner and the relationship had flourished.

Chapter 6

It was several months before Tianne and Patti spoke again. Tianne had travelled extensively with Rashid to Cairo and other Middle Eastern and European countries although she was not fully aware of his clandestine involvements. As a Muslim wife she was not informed of her husband's activities as it was not a woman's concern.

'We're in Athens, Mother,' Tianne said excitedly over the phone, 'and we just got married!'

Patti couldn't believe what she was hearing. 'What?'

'We were married, in a registry office. It was wonderful!'

'But he's already married,' Patti shouted over the phone.

'He's Muslim and his religion allows him to have more than one wife,' Tianne replied patiently as if she was speaking to a child. 'We're going back to London for a while and then on to Australia. He needs a passport and he can travel on mine. He has to get into the UK and Australia so this is perfect for him. He needs my help, Mother.'

'But what about you?' Patti almost screamed. 'Your marriage won't be recognised in England or Australia. He'll be classified as a bigamist! You haven't turned Muslim, have you?' Patti asked in dread.

Tianne laughed. 'Don't be silly, Mother, of course I haven't. I've met his wife and children. There's no love lost there, Mother. It's over.'

'That's not the point! It's not legal!' Another thought occurred to her. 'You went to Cairo to meet his wife and kids?' Patti yelled uncontrollably.

'No, his wife and kids live in Cyprus.'

'But he told me they were…'

But Tianne interrupted her. 'Don't worry, Mum, we'll be fine. We'll be in the same business so we can help one another just like you and Dennis. I told you, he needs to travel on my passport. He needs my help and I do love him.'

'But Tianne, think this through,' Patti begged. 'I grant you he's gorgeous but that's not enough. He's very immature and apparently, so are you. This is ridiculous. You're throwing your life away! Leave him and come back to Australia. You know we have to leave Cyprus and move back otherwise Immigration won't allow us back in.'

Immigration laws had changed when Bob Hawke came to power as Australian Prime Minister and whereas Australian and British passport holders were formerly allowed to travel freely between the two countries, ex-pats now had to apply to the Immigration Department to re-enter Australia.

Deciding to return home to Australia Patti and Dennis discovered they would now require permission. They applied but were refused. Tianne assured them that she could fix their problem and set about the task. Patti and Dennis had no idea how she managed it but, true to her word, she somehow succeeded but Patti and Dennis would have to leave Cyprus urgently. After eight years of living as ex-pats overseas they could return home.

Tianne laughed. 'After we make our fortune in England we'll come back, I promise. Gotta go. I'll be in touch when we get to England.'

Tianne hung up the phone leaving Patti yelling, 'Tianne! Tianne, listen to me!'

But Tianne was young, impetuous and in love, which gave her the confidence that she could handle anything in life. Unfortunately she couldn't.

Patti and Dennis left Cyprus and returned to Australia where Dennis was offered the job at the 'Top of the State' in Queensland. Brisbane was in the grip of the exciting and hugely successful Commonwealth Games, and accommodation was very expensive and scarce. They headed further out into the country and discovered a delightful property in the lovely secluded little village of Crow's Nest on the Darling Downs just outside the city of Toowoomba. They fell in love with the peacefulness of the area and despite the two-hour drive from Brisbane, decided to buy there.

Chapter 7

Patti again didn't hear from Tianne for several weeks until she received a phone call from her closest friend and fellow performer, Maggie Hall. Maggie rang her to say she'd heard through a mutual friend that Tianne and Rashid had returned to Australia and were living in Cairns. This was an inexcusable surprise to Patti who couldn't understand why Tianne hadn't contacted her. Maggie was able to enlighten her on that point. Tianne was apparently too embarrassed to ring her mother as things weren't turning out too well with Rashid or their marriage. She reported that apparently Rashid had beaten Tianne in Cairns and was arrested for domestic violence but he had been placed on a good behaviour bond when Tianne refused to lay charges. It would appear Rashid had taken to losing his temper quite often and lashing out at Tianne, physically. It was said that he had punched her in the face while they were living in Kensington in London and Tianne had to be admitted to hospital with a cut cheek and a black and swollen eye. He had been arrested, charged and served three months but Tianne refused to lay charges claiming the row had been her fault. He apologised but accused Tianne of instigating the incident by throwing a banana at him in a rage. Theatre or television work had not been forthcoming and Tianne had taken up teaching drama to young school children in London to support them.

Rashid claimed being a Muslim gave him the right to discipline his wife as she was his property. Apparently the relationship had become pretty stormy with many outbursts of temper on both sides interspersed with times of passionate reconciliation.

Although not entirely surprised, Patti was horrified at this news and lived in fear for her daughter's welfare and safety. She asked if Maggie knew where Tianne could be reached so she could bring her daughter home and care for her. Unfortunately Maggie wasn't able to help as she'd only heard the news from an intermediary and didn't know if the details were true or just gossip. This did little to pacify Patti's concerns but apart from appealing to the police, which would lead to further contention, there was little she could do.

Next she heard that the couple had left Cairns and settled in an apartment in the Brisbane suburb of Paddington but there was still no direct contact with Tianne. Eventually Tianne rang from Brisbane, sobbing, and in a frantic state. Patti had never seen or heard her daughter cry as she always appeared in control of any situation. She said Rashid had physically attacked her in Edward Street, in the city, and roughly dragged her along by her arm but passersby would not interfere in what was an obvious domestic situation; nobody interfered in domestic disputes at that time. Eventually a passing priest intervened, admonished Rashid, and took Tianne to a nunnery where she would be protected by the nuns.

'Listen to me, Tianne,' Patti instructed her. 'Give me your address and stay right where you are, we're coming down to get you.'

Dennis had lost patience with the whole affair and at first refused to become involved. 'She brought this on herself, Patti, she knew what she was getting into. She's an adult, for God's sake, she's got to stand up for herself and fight her own battles. I've had enough. Bring her here and I'll move out.'

'But Dennis, she's living with a psychopath, the man's a monster. If I could drive I'd go by myself but I can't and she's my only daughter. She's never asked for my help before and I'm not going to abandon her. I'd never forgive myself if anything happened to her.'

'What about the time she got caught up in that nutty religious cult in Australia while we were living in England? She asked for your help then and you managed to get her out of that.'

'That was different,' Patti said. 'She wasn't in physical danger.'

Finally and reluctantly, Dennis agreed and they drove to Brisbane.

Patti stayed in the car while Dennis collected Tianne from the nuns and they drove to Paddington to collect Tianne's belongings. Again Patti stayed in the car in case Rashid objected to her interference. When Rashid opened the door to Tianne and Dennis he smiled charmingly, ignored Tianne completely and shook Dennis's hand.

'I believe you enjoy beating women up,' Dennis said, coldly. 'Do it again and I'll have you deported.'

Rashid replied with that smile and said, 'Misunderstanding, Dennis, you know what women are like.'

However, he allowed Tianne to collect her belongings and leave with Dennis and they returned to Crow's Nest.

Tianne was silent but obviously still distraught on the trip back and when they arrived in Crow's Nest. She had lost a lot of weight and seemed to have bronchitis. For some time she wouldn't talk about her problems but Patti noticed she spent a lot of time during the days and nights silently sitting on the back porch deep in thought or sleeping. It was like she was in a trance. Finally, unable to stand the tension any longer, Patti joined her on the porch and placed her hand on her daughter's shoulder.

'You've got to talk to me, Tianne, I'm your mother and I love you.'

And the floodgates opened.

'I've been such a fool, Mum,' Tianne wailed. 'He's so possessive. He's terribly jealous, he won't let me have any friends of my own, he follows me everywhere and he even smashed in the bathroom door when I locked it. He rips my crucifixes from my neck and throws them on the ground and stamps his heel on them. He pushes my face into the mirror and tells me how ugly I am. It's just terrible.'

'My God, you've got to get out. Leave him, Tianne. He'll bring you nothing but disaster,' Patti pleaded.

'You don't understand. He'll never let me go. He owns me. It's not that easy, Mum,' Tianne said quietly. 'When he behaves himself he's wonderful – charming, romantic, caring, loving. The reconciliations are wonderful and I do love him. It's just that he has such a terrible temper that he can't control. The smallest thing can set him off. I thought I could change him.'

'You can't change men like that, Tianne, they have to want to change themselves and I don't think that's going to happen with Rashid. He's completely self-absorbed. No one exists in his world but him. Does he still abuse you, I mean hit you?

Tianne paused before she answered. 'He's only hit me a couple of times and a lot of that was my fault. I push him too far. Muslim men won't stand for that.'

There was another long pause and Tianne quietly spoke. 'He's killed people, Mother, he was in the army for a sort of National Service in Lebanon. He claimed he'd killed.' She paused and looked Patti in the face. 'He also boasted to me that he'd killed a married couple who had insulted him.'

Patti was aghast.

'I didn't believe him and told him he might have killed the woman but he'd never kill a man as he was a coward. That was one of the times he hit me. I should never have said he was a coward.'

Patti frowned in horror at this admission. 'You've got to get out, Tianne, anyone can disappear if they try. Take a plane back to England, go to America, anywhere. Get out while you can!'

'He'll find me,' Tianne said simply. 'I know other things about him. He'll never let me go.'

After five days, Tianne seemed calmer and resigned to leaving Rashid. She decided to go back to Brisbane and stay with a friend who had offered her a room while she considered what to do.

Patti wasn't convinced returning to Brisbane was a good idea but Tianne was determined, claiming she wasn't going to let Rashid run her life.

Patti walked her to the bus and as it arrived, quite out of character for mother and daughter, they embraced, warmly. There seemed nothing else to say to each other. Patti watched as Tianne walked towards the bus and stopped and turned. She gave her mother the most beautiful smile, boarded the bus and it drove away.

Chapter 8

Sergeant Lyle asked Patti if she would accompany him to the local police station for an interview. He was very gentle. He'd been on the force for over thirty years but telling someone their child had been murdered never got easier. After the initial shock, Patti's mind was numb.

At the police station, Lyle handed her a very large Scotch. This was not the usual thing but he figured she would need it for the details he was about to give her.

'I only saw her six days ago,' Patti whispered disbelievingly.

'Your daughter was strangled on the eleventh of October, Mrs Price,' he said gently, 'but I'm afraid she'd been beaten very severely about the head approximately four or five hours beforehand. It was a particularly vicious beating, I'm afraid. Your daughter put up a brave fight.'

'Are you sure it's her?' Patti said, daring to hope. 'I mean if she was so badly beaten…'

'It took us three days to identify her. Your ex-husband contacted us when he saw her photo on television. He identified her.'

'Oh, poor Mike,' Patti sobbed. 'It must've been horrendous for him. I don't think I could've done it.'

What was not known was that Rashid had hired a car and driven them down to Jupiter's Casino on the Gold Coast, which they had frequently visited. They separated and gambled but the poker machines weren't very kind to Tianne that night and she soon lost the money she was carrying. She found Rashid and asked him for some of the money he owed her and he refused. A heated argument started and eventually he seemed to renege and told her he'd left some money in the car and he'd go out and get it. Suspecting he would drive off and leave her there, which was quite within his character, she insisted on accompanying him. They left the casino and headed for the almost empty parking area. It was late at night by this stage and the car park was almost deserted. She stood by the car as he went to open the boot. Still berating him, she joined him at the rear of the car. In a rage and refusing to take her abuse any longer, he raised his fist and violently punched her in the face, she tried to fight back but he continued punching her violently. Fury turned to blind frenzy as he grabbed a tyre lever from the boot of the car and swung it at her, catching her on the side of her head with a heavy blow. She fell to the ground, unconscious.

Alarmed and frantically looking around to make sure there were no witnesses, he lifted her body from the ground, pushed her into the boot of the car and slammed the door shut. He suddenly remembered some plastic ties he carried in the car in case of an emergency. Again checking they were alone, he quickly opened the boot of the car, grabbed the ties and secured Tianne's hands in case she regained consciousness and started to struggle and scream. In a panic, suspecting he may even have possibly killed her, he threw himself into the driver's seat, started the engine and roared out of the car park.

He drove back to Brisbane forming his plan on the way. Arriving at the apartment they shared in Paddington he phoned the coffee shop where he and his friends met to plan demonstrations and asked to speak to Abs. Without going into detail he quickly told Abs that he needed his help urgently and to come over to the apartment on his motorbike. He then quickly collected all of their personal possessions, even including Tianne's toothbrush and shampoo, and threw them into the car. Tianne was lying very quiet and still and he assumed that he had killed her. Peter, their flatmate who shared the apartment with them, heard Rashid come home and pretended he was asleep when Rashid entered his room to collect any personal items he may have left there. Peter was very frightened of Rashid having witnessed some of the violent arguments he'd had with Tianne.

Abs arrived and followed Rashid as he drove off in the direction of the M1 motorway, planning to dispose of her body somewhere on his trip south.

But when he reached Carrara he suddenly heard yelling and kicking coming from the boot of the car. He turned off at the next exit and pulled in near the golf course which was devoid of traffic. Abs followed close behind and parked his bike a little distance away. Rashid flung open the boot and saw that Tianne had recovered consciousness. She screamed and kicked out at him. He dragged her from the car her heels leaving indentations in the ground and hit her several more times as she struggled and fought desperately. She had strong dancer's legs and used them to kick out at him but he evaded most of her attacks and continued to bash her head and body furiously. Tianne noticed Abs parked nearby and screamed, 'Help me, help me!' But Abs remained sitting on his bike and did not come to her aid. Rashid grabbed her throat and crushed her windpipe to stop her screaming. He squeezed until she stopped struggling and lay still. He had finished the job and Tianne was dead.

Panting from the exertion, his fury spent, he slowly stood and looked down at her beaten, dead body almost sadly. Leaving her body where it lay, he returned to the driver's seat and drove off. Abs kicked the motor of his bike into action and followed but took the exit back to Brisbane. Rashid continued south.

At the police station, Patti, deep in shock, nodded numbly, all the time thinking, Rashid… Rashid did this… I warned her, I warned her.

'We don't think robbery was involved,' Sergeant Lyle continued. 'They found a gold watch and a little cash nearby. It would appear your daughter had been driven to the spot. They also found tyre track marks near the body. There was no sign of sexual assault.'

Horrific words, words, words without real meaning assailed her being. The full realisation would come later and the horror would never leave her.

'We believe she had been seen with a man at Jupiter's Casino earlier in the evening,' Lyle continued. 'There'd apparently been an argument. Your daughter and the man left together. Do you have any idea who that man might be, Mrs Price?'

Patti had no doubt who that man had been. 'Rashid... I assume. It was her bigamous husband, Rashid El Parviz. He killed her. I have no doubt. He's an Iranian but prefers to be known as a Persian – more exotic,' she said bitterly. 'They'd been recently separated. He is a monster, Detective Sergeant, an absolute monster.'

'We'll look into that, Mrs Price,' he said jotting down the name. 'We always start with the husband or boyfriend. Can you tell me where we might find this Rashid El Parviz?'

'I have an address in Paddington where they were living.'

Her hands shaking, she took a small address book from her handbag, found the entry and handed it to the policeman.

'Please find him, Sergeant,' she begged. 'You must find him and bring him to justice. I'll never rest until he's dead or behind bars for the rest of his life.'

'We'll do our best Mrs Price, I can assure you. If he's still at this address he'll be brought in for questioning.'

But he wasn't at that address. He'd moved out apparently on the morning after the murder, according to their flatmate who had heard the car leave, apparently taking all his and Tianne's personal belongings with him. An alert was issued to all states and airports to apprehend him for questioning on the murder of Tianne Allen Kelly.

Thinking he had probably left the state, Patti remembered a friend in Melbourne who had been one of her bridesmaids at her first wedding and who knew where Rashid and Tianne had stayed when they passed through Melbourne on the way from England, and rang her. Her friend remembered the address and gave it to Patti who then passed it on to the police.

It took a few days before Rashid was apprehended in Melbourne. The police had staked out the address Patti had given them, waited and followed him when he left the premises. He was encircled by a ring of police and arrested outside a travel agent's office in Little Collins Street where he had attempted to purchase a ticket to Limassol under a false name. He'd asked if the attendant could make the ticket out in the name of Youssef as he didn't want to be identified, which of course was against the law, and was promptly refused.

On questioning he acted remarkably calm even when told of his wife's murder and claimed the police were lying. They showed him a photo of her dead body. He completely denied any involvement saying he had left Tianne and was returning to

Cyprus. His story was he had indeed been with Tianne at Jupiter's Casino on the night of her murder but had left her after an argument with her over another man she was with whom he described as dark and tall with a moustache. He claimed she was a slut and that's why they'd argued and he'd walked out on her saying he'd see her in Melbourne. He claimed he returned home to their flat in Paddington, packed up their belongings and caught a bus to Melbourne where he had friends who would take care of them until they found a place of their own.

Surprisingly, the yellow Mazda Rashid had hired in Brisbane and was seen driving the night of the murder turned up in the hire car's Melbourne office three days after the murder, the same day he said he'd arrived by bus. When confronted with this information under questioning, he admitted he'd driven the car down and lied about the bus trip because he thought that's what the police wanted him to say. Further investigation proved that the tyre tracks found near the murder scene matched the tyre treads on the hired Mazda.

Rashid El Parviz was arrested for murder. An open-and-shut case?

Chapter 9

Tianne's body was held by the Medical Examiner for two weeks before it was released. The autopsy showed she had died by strangulation approximately four hours after severe trauma to the neck, head, face and body. It also showed she was suffering from pneumonia. The face was almost unrecognisable.

Rashid was held in prison for twelve months before the case came to trial. During that time he solicited help from three other inmates to provide him with an alibi.

Unexpectedly The Insignificant Man, his handler, arrived at the jail to visit Rashid.

'Well, you certainly made your mark this time, young man,' the handler said as they sat in the holding cell.

'I'll get off,' Rashid replied confidently. 'I've been in worse spots.'

'Not in Australia, my friend,' the handler responded. 'They don't take well to wife-killing in

Australia. Luckily it's not the Middle East though. As a good Muslim boy her family would demand a revenge killing if you were found guilty.'

'She wasn't a Muslim,' Rashid reminded him, 'but her mother would probably kill me if she got the chance. But I can take care of her. I have a good network here.'

The handler didn't respond immediately and just sat looking at him with his usual unreadable expression. 'I think you've done enough,' he finally said.

'Besides,' Rashid continued, 'your intelligence mob have got a lot at stake here. It wouldn't look good if it came out that I was a double agent for them, would it?'

'I'm sure they will do all in their power to avoid that,' the handler replied coolly, 'even if it meant your meeting with an unfortunate accident while you're in here.'

Rashid took that in and smiled. 'I don't see that happening,' he smirked. 'I have written records of our dealings hidden away with my friends here in the Sunshine State. If anything were to happen to me...' he left the sentence unfinished.

The Insignificant Man's expression didn't change.

One of the inmates Rashid approached in prison, Michael Carter, had asked him what he was in for and Rashid replied, 'Murdering my wife.'

'And did you do it?' Michael asked.

'Yeah, I killed the bitch,' admitted Rashid. 'She was crazy. They won't get me for it. I need an alibi.'

'You'd be better off going for a plea,' replied Carter. 'Just tell 'em you lost control and she was attacking you and you might get it downgraded to manslaughter for self defence.'

'No, I want out of this fuckin' place. I won't do time. I want an alibi,' Rashid repeated defiantly. 'I can get heroin if you're interested.''

'When did you do it?' asked Carter.

'Twelfth of October,' Rashid mumbled, checking to see they weren't being overheard.

'Can't help ya, mate, I was in here at that time. Ask around, maybe someone'll help ya, for a price. Wouldn't count on it though, ya get almost as much for perjury if they catch you as if ya actually did the crime. Ya never know though, some o' the bastards in here are pretty desperate.'

Rashid approached another inmate, Steve Collins, who had only recently been incarcerated for rape and robbery with violence with an accomplice, Trevor Manders, and put the proposition to him. Steve thought about it and said he'd get back to him.

A day later, Steve approached him in the sick bay where Rashid had been placed for suspected hepatitis. Steve sidled up to him and whispered, 'Me an' me mate Trev are up for it if you can come up with the stuff. We'll give evidence we were all together at the pub an' went back to your place an' got pissed an' stayed the night.'

Rashid was elated and said he'd arrange for the stuff through a 'friend'.

Patti actually needed to come face to face with her daughter's killer and arranged for a visit. With heart pounding, she steeled herself for the upcoming ordeal.

She was searched and escorted to a small interview room with a large window. Behind the plate-glass window, at a bench, Rashid sat in jeans and a white T-shirt. Patti remained standing. He looked ill. She'd been told he was suffering from hepatitis B and had actually bitten another inmate in a dispute. He told the other inmate that he was now infected with AIDS.

They stared silently at each other for a long time sizing each other up before Rashid said, 'I consented to see you.'

Patti choked in revulsion but managed to say, 'Why did you kill my daughter?'

Rashid's cold black eyes stared into hers. 'Now you care,' he said with a cruel smile.

'Did you ever love her?' Patti asked, the bile rising in her throat.

'Of course,' he said smiling, but the smile died before it reached his black eyes. 'I can't sleep. I have nightmares about her. She keeps calling out for me to help her.'

She stared at him in disbelief, waiting for him to attempt to justify himself, but frigid silence reigned between them.

'How could you ever have loved her?' she spat at him. 'You fooled her into marrying you, you fought with her, you insulted her, you hit her, you threw her into the boot of the car and drove her around for hours before you dragged her out of the car with her hands tied. You beat her mercilessly until she was unrecognisable and then you strangled her and left her poor battered body in the dirt.'

He continued to stare coldly at her.

Appalled, and her venom spent, Patti took a step backwards. 'You lied,' she said. 'You lie to me, you lied to Tianne, you lied to the police, you lied to your wife and children, you lie to everyone. And you'll lie to the court and the jury. You deserve to hang.'

He continued to stare at her but his eyes shifted slightly and they now showed contempt and hate.

It was too much for Patti as loathing, frustration and horror enveloped her being as she stared at the hands and into the eyes of the man who had beaten and strangled her daughter to death; the hands and eyes that were probably the last thing her daughter had seen before she died horribly. The storm within her broke and she sobbed uncontrollably as she opened the door and fled from the room. Rashid simply stared after her.

Chapter 10

The Insignificant Man sat at a desk in a private office in Roma Street Police Station opposite his superior officer, Robert Rawlins.

Rawlins was a man in late middle age, plump with a fleshy face that settled into deep wrinkles in repose and deep thought, which was almost constantly. His fair hair was thinning with a receding hairline, his body plump due to lack of exercise and a taste for Fourex beer and the wrong foods. But his mind was razor sharp.

He was dressed in a pale grey suit, the jacket of which hung over the back of his office chair leaving him in slacks, a bright white business shirt and grey silk tie. His fingers steepled together as if in prayer, almost touching the tip of his more than adequate nose, his face now in repose, his grey eyes fixed in a thoughtful stare over The Insignificant Man's head.

'So, how are we going to handle this?' The Insignificant Man asked. 'He's obviously gone rogue and landed us in a very…' he paused, 'delicate situation.'

'And he claims he's got records that could be an embarrassment to the department if they're released,' Rawlins replied.

'Hmmm. And he has his connections with the PLO and the Muslim Youth Organisation he helped to set up. Could get nasty on many fronts.'

Rawlins nodded and continued to think.

'We have an undercover mole in his Youth Group that operates out of a coffee shop in Albion,' the agent continued. 'He keeps us up to date on planned demonstrations and information coming out of the PLO. The group's pretty much under control.'

'So we'll have to cover for the mongrel for the time being and get him out of the country I suppose,' Rawlins postulated. 'Could be very tricky but not entirely impossible with the right connections. Lot of effort. You sure he did it?'

The Insignificant Man nodded. 'Almost certain.'

'I need definite,' Rawlins demanded, 'if I'm going to stick our necks out…'

The agent paused. 'Yeah, it's definite.'

'Bloody feral,' Rawlins said in disgust. 'We need something else – some evidence to hold over his head if things go wrong. Find me something. When this is over, we never use him again but we'll keep a close eye on the bastard. Is that clear?'

'Perfectly.' The agent paused. 'Maybe he can meet with an accident in another country?'

Rawlins nodded. 'Could raise issues if it happened in Australia.' He continued in deep thought weighing up the possibilities. 'I'll have to go further up the line for assistance. Call in some favours. Maybe an inept barrister; that shouldn't be too difficult; one who can be manipulated, maybe one from out of town.' His eyes narrowed in thought. 'We may have to tamper with the jury a bit, play around with the evidence maybe.' He thought for a while longer. 'The Fitzgerald inquiry might actually come in handy as a matter of fact.' The brain continued to tick over.

The Insignificant Man stood preparing to leave. 'Anything you want me to do?'

'I'll get back to you,' Rawlins replied. 'Keep me posted.' He pointed a demanding finger at his agent. 'And get me that evidence.'

Chapter 11

The cemetery was crowded with show business friends dressed, at Patti's request, in bright-coloured clothes in honour of the memory of her fun-loving, extrovert daughter. Patti was completely numb and would never remember exactly who or how many mourners were there. At the rear and on the outskirts of the mourners The Insignificant Man stood watching.

Despite his detached expression, in his heart he felt a great sadness and sympathy for Patti as he watched her standing by her daughter's grave, alone in her grief, and completely oblivious to her surroundings. Her husband, Dennis, stood beside her. He did not have his arm around her or try to console her. It would not have helped if he had.

Later, at the wake, which the agent did not attend, Patti steeled herself and read a poem Tianne had written to the assembled guests.

'N when you're feeling low

Raise your soul high

To the Universal oneness of you and I

Feeling isolated in a land of foreign minds

I look to a stranger sky

'N I know Christ never really did die

So let your love rub out your cries

'N when you're feeling low

Raise your soul high.

The Insignificant Man had two daughters that he loved dearly and could only imagine the hurt and despair Patti was going through. There was no doubt he was responsible for bringing Tianne and Rashid together. He'd done some pretty questionable things in his career but that came with the intelligence territory. Rashid had provided some useful bits of information and been fed other secrets that the department wanted to get back to the PLO but not at the cost of a beautiful woman's life. In his heart he was determined that although he would follow orders and help in any way to gain an acquittal for the murderer, he would also do all in his power to make sure the killer would pay for his callous crime; maybe not now but at sometime in the future.

He and Rawlins had done some pretty outrageous things in an attempt to secure the verdict that was necessary for the good of the country and to save the Department from unwelcome scrutiny, publicity and embarrassment but nothing could be guaranteed.

He believed he had managed, at great personal risk, to obtain the solid evidence Rawlins had demanded, which could be held over Rashid's head for the rest of his life, but being forced to release it could have other grave consequences. Like much information gathered by the clandestine intelligence agencies, evidence was often a double-edged sword.

Chapter 12

The Trial

Not surprisingly for such a high profile case, the courtroom was packed. There was a large proportion of Palestinians and Middle-Eastern migrants in the crowd who jostled for the best seats. The Insignificant Man sat on the aisle in the second back row watching the proceedings. Patti had been called to give evidence and sat on a bench outside the courtroom waiting to be summoned but irritatingly, for some unknown reason, she was not called and could not hear how the case was progressing. This was probably because the defence counsel may have argued that the jury might be compromised, moved by the sight of the beautiful, grieving, high-profile mother of the victim. For two days she sat there and was never called to give evidence.

Several witnesses were called by the Crown prosecutor, the relatively low-profile Joshua Delaney, who was originally from New Zealand and who had lost many cases in the past. The police officer in charge and chief investigator of the case, Detective Sergeant Porter, gave evidence of the crime scene and the details of Rashid's arrest. He also related that a prisoner, Michael Carter, who was incarcerated with Rashid in Boggo Road Jail prior to the trial, told him that Rashid had confessed to his wife's murder saying, 'Yes, I killed the bitch.. According to Porter, Rashid then asked Carter if he would provide an alibi for him in return for money and drugs. Carter refused saying he advised Rashid to confess to a lesser charge of self-defence and manslaughter.

Rashid sat in the dock, immaculately dressed and looking handsome, vulnerable, sad and confused, shaking his head at each accusation.

Porter also described evidence found at the scene of the crime which included tyre tracks similar to the tyres on the hire car Rashid had hired in Brisbane. He was seen driving the car on the night of the murder and the vehicle later turned up in Melbourne. Also, the struggle marks found on the ground beside and under the body, the sighting of Tianne and a man of similar appearance to Rashid at Jupiter's Casino arguing on the night of the murder, and the scratches found on Rashid's face when he was apprehended in Melbourne were stated in evidence.

Unbelievably there was no mention of any residue being found under Tianne's fingernails linking Rashid as her assailant.

Samples had been sent for testing but they had mysteriously disappeared in transit and no forensic report was ever received or discovered. Therefore the lack of physical evidence was inadmissible. Patti was astounded when the evidence was virtually dismissed in the court. She followed the Medical Examiner out of the courtroom and confronted him on the footpath demanding an explanation. He was obviously embarrassed and looked down at his feet unable to meet her eyes.

'They were lost,' he mumbled and quickly shuffled off to a waiting car leaving Patti shocked and open mouthed in incredulity.

In reply and cross examination the Defence counsel pointed out that Rashid had not been definitely identified as the man at the Casino arguing with Tianne and submitted that Rashid had claimed Tianne was with another man at the time of the argument who was of similar appearance, tall, slim and dark but with a moustache. The man in question had never been identified or apprehended. Porter had also claimed that Rashid and Tianne were seen leaving the casino together and submitted the prosecution's theory that he had bashed and killed the victim and thrown her into their car and driven off but the defence claimed it was purely circumstantial and could not be proved as there were no witnesses. Besides, the medical evidence stated that Tianne had been killed four or five hours later than she had been seen leaving the casino by which time Rashid's car was seen on his way back to Brisbane.

With a copy of the Quran clutched in his hand like a faithful Muslim, Rashid turned towards the jury helplessly and shook his head at the accusations made against him.

Counsel for the prosecution established there was strong evidence that the couple's relationship had broken down dramatically during the weeks leading up to the murder and a female witness and former friend of Rashid's, Jolie Macklin, claimed under oath that Rashid had spoken to her often about killing his wife when Rashid visited her flat in New Farm, telling her, 'I feel the only way to get her out of my life is to kill her.' She also claimed he had told her he had tried to kill his wife once before saying, 'I drove her up Tamborine Mountain. I was going to strangle her. I was so close to putting my hands around her neck but then I saw an old man watching us and knew if I strangled her then I would be seen so I didn't do it.'

Ms Macklin also said Rashid had offered to kill a man for her if she wanted; a man with whom she had been involved in a car accident. 'It's all right,' she claimed he'd said, 'I know how to kill. I've done it before. I was in the Palestinian Army and you learn how to do these things.'

'Lies, lies,' Rashid screamed from the defence table.

'Order in the court,' the judge demanded loudly.

Patti knew Detective Sergeant Porter had also interviewed Peter Ryde who was staying as a flatmate at the Paddington address at the time of the murder. At first he said he pretended to be asleep in his room when Rashid entered the room at about midnight. Having witnessed Rashid's violent behaviour towards Tianne on several occasions, Ryde was afraid of him and said nothing as Rashid cleaned out any personal effects and left the room. Later, Ryde claimed, he heard Rashid drive away. When Detective Sergeant Porter tried to re-interview Ryde again later on and call him as a witness, Ryde had disappeared and left for an overseas trip that had already lasted over a year.

The detective sergeant's evidence of that account was therefore inadmissible.

Father James Sullivan gave evidence that he had seen Rashid assaulting and pushing Tianne violently down Edward Street in the city and had rescued her and threatened Rashid with citizen's arrest if he did not cease his attack. Rashid stormed off and the priest had taken Tianne to a home run by the Saint Joseph Sisters for her personal protection.

On the third day of the trial, Patti was at last allowed to enter the courtroom, not as a witness but as a spectator. Before the court came to session, Patti was outside with a crowd of people waiting for admission when she was approached by a little old Palestinian woman who obviously did not know who Patti was, and who asked her how she thought the trial was going. Patti replied that she thought it was going quite well to which the old lady replied sadly, 'That poor boy, with that beautiful innocent face. He couldn't hurt a cockroach. He can hardly speak English and he doesn't understand what's going on. We have to do everything to help him.'

Patti later found out the Palestine Youth Movement or the infamous PLO of which Rashid was a member was paying for his legal costs.

After the prosecutor had completed his case, an attractive young woman barrister, Anna Woodrow, opened her case for the defence claiming the prosecution case was all based on circumstantial evidence. She submitted that there was no blood, fibres or hair found in the car when it was examined by the forensic department.

As to the tyre tracks discovered at the scene, she submitted that the tyres were of a very common and popular brand and that over 100,000 sets of these tyres had been sold in Queensland and NSW. Besides, owing to the lack of any soil in the tyre tracks being found when the car had been examined in Melbourne, it could not be proved this was the car at the murder scene.

The prosecution remarked that it was very coincidental that the same tyres were found on the car Rashid was driving and that the car had been cleaned probably both by Rashid and the car company after it was returned in Melbourne. It had been hired by other drivers after it had been returned and before it was discovered by the police and therefore any evidence would be compromised. But the point had been made.

It was admitted that Rashid had been arrested in Cairns for domestic violence against his wife but that she had instigated the assault by attacking him physically and insulting him and he was protecting himself. It was noted that she had never brought formal charges against him, he had never been imprisoned and they had reconciled and continued living together. Was that the sign of a serial wife basher and wife killer?

The defence counsel then called two male witnesses, Steven Collins and Trevor Manders, who gave evidence that they had been with Rashid at a nightclub in Fortitude Valley on the night of the murder and that he had been distraught because he had argued with his wife who had been flirting with another man at the Casino. They had all driven home to Rashid's apartment, got hopelessly drunk and stayed the night.

The Crown submitted in reply that both men had criminal records and had been incarcerated with Rashid prior to the trial and their evidence should be strongly questioned.

Under cross-examination Detective Sergeant Porter was asked if he had worked on the Jeffrey Maddox case. Joshua Delaney jumped to his feet and objected as the question was irrelevant. The judge quickly overruled the defence counsel and disallowed the question.

The Jeffrey Maddox case had recently been a very controversial case when Maddox had been charged and had supposedly confessed to the murder of his father. The defence had claimed Maddox had been bullied and coerced in his confession by the police who had threatened Maddox with charging members of his family as accomplices if he didn't confess. The case against Maddox was dropped.

At the time of the trial, the Queensland Police Force was wracked by the current Fitzgerald Crime and Corruption Inquiry in which, among many other claims, police were being accused of bribery and tampering with witnesses and evidence to gain a conviction. The police sergeant who was first on the scene of Tianne's murder was one of the policemen under investigation. The general public had become suspicious of any police involvement in an investigation.

A Catholic priest, Father Flynn, who served at the prison, was then called in Rashid's defence. He stated that Rashid, in his opinion, seemed to be a fine, spiritual and religious man who was a proud Muslim, whose culture and religion admittedly differed from the Australian way by allowing multiple wives and the disciplining of his wives as the wife was considered to be property. He stated that Rashid appeared genuinely distraught at the murder of his wife and because of his difficulty with the English language, was confused with the legal process of the trial.

That night, physically and mentally exhausted, Patti was just dropping off to sleep when she suddenly had a dream, or was it a vision? – of Tianne smiling at her. Patti suddenly felt as if she was being strangled and realised that Tianne was trying to show her how she'd died. She felt Rashid's hands, tight around her throat, choking her and felt she was staring up into his hate-twisted, manic face and those cold, black eyes.

She heard Tianne screaming, 'Help me, please help me.'

But who was she screaming for help to? Certainly not Rashid.

Then she thought she saw Rashid stand, look down at her and walk away. But she also saw the figure of another man, from the back, short and very stocky, dressed in a distinctive black and purple leather jacket sitting on a motorcycle, driving away after Rashid. In a panic she called out Tianne's name and woke.

On the fifth day of the trial, Rashid took the stand and definitely centre stage.

Chapter 13

The judge pointed out to the jury that Rashid was under no legal obligation to give evidence at his own trial but had volunteered to do so.

This was Rashid's chance for a Royal Command Performance. When called to the stand he glanced towards the jury and gave a sad, defeated smile. He entered the witness box clutching the Quran and swore the oath and continued looking toward the jurors. In response to his counsel's first question as to the validity of the charge, Rashid again turned to the jury.

'Please,' Rashid pleaded, 'I not kill Tianne, I loved her, I would never do anything like that! I swear on God! I not a violent man. I never hit anyone. I discipline but no hurt. I no understand! Please, you believe me, please!'

His normally very proficient English obviously had abandoned him and he had reverted to a heavily accented, intermittent, staggered speech.

The judge called for order and instructed Rashid not to address the jury directly. 'I no even hurt my pussycat when she scratch me on face,' he continued, leaning forward and holding out his arms to the jurors and pointing to the scars from the scratches Tianne had inflicted on him during their struggle.

He was again ordered to be silent until the counsel questioned him and he responded by breaking down in real tears and sobbing pitifully.

It had an astounding effect on the whole courtroom.

Maggie leaned in to Patti and whispered, 'He's good, he's damned good.'

Patti frowned and nodded her head.

Any question put to Rashid was either haltingly answered or elicited a helpless, 'I sorry. I no understand.'

It was now the prosecutor's opportunity to cross examine.

'And why did you attempt to leave Australia three days after your wife's murder, Mr Parviz, after having only just arrived in Melbourne from Brisbane?'

'I not know she dead,' Rashid replied. 'Victoria too cold. I wanted go back to Cyprus to my wife and family.'

'And why did you lie to the police telling them that you caught a bus to Melbourne when in fact you drove a hire car?'

'I thought that was what the policeman wanted me to say and they would let me go,' Rashid replied.

The counsellor looked askance. 'Why would the police ask you to lie?'

Rashid shrugged uncomprehendingly.

The prosecutor shook his head in amazement. 'I doubt it was the police lying, Mr Parviz. Isn't it true that you argued with your wife at Jupiter's Casino on the night of the murder and later drove her to Carrara where you brutally bashed and strangled her?' he demanded, to which Rashid replied again directly to the jury, 'Nooooo!' he sobbed.

The judge stopped proceedings and once again instructed Rashid to face counsel when answering questions and to please try and control his emotions.

The judge asked if he would feel more at ease with an interpreter and Rashid refused saying haltingly, 'No, thank you, I speak good English.'

The judge raised his eyebrows in disbelief and invited the prosecutor to continue.

'And is it not a fact, Mr Parviz, that you already had a wife and two children in Cyprus when you married the victim in Athens?'

'Yes, but I am Muslim and my religion allows me more than one wife.'

'Australia is not a Muslim country, Mr Parviz, most of us consider one wife more than sufficient,' Delaney replied, which elicited a much-needed laugh from the gallery.

'I needed to marry a Western woman to allow me to enter Australia. Tianne knew this when we married,' Rashid responded as if this was perfectly natural.

This drew a muttering from the gallery, the Middle-Eastern contingent in favour of his statement and the Australian element dubious.

'And where are your wife and two small children residing now, Mr Parviz?

Rashid shrugged and again turned to the jury with a pleading expression. 'They still live in Cyprus. They miss me. I wish to return there, please, they need me to look after them.'

'Perhaps you should've thought of that before you entered this farcical bigamous marriage,' Delaney responded.

This drew an objection from the Defence counsel. The judge sustained the objection but again reminded Rashid not to talk directly to the jury. Delaney withdrew the statement, apologised and moved on.

'What is your occupation, Mr Parviz?' asked the prosecutor.

'Pardon?' Rashid replied.

'Your occupation,' the prosecutor repeated slowly and distinctly.

'I am an actor,' Rashid mumbled softly.

'Louder, please, Mr Parviz,' the judge ordered.

'An actor,' Rashid replied loudly.

'An actor? I'd say you were very good at your craft, Mr Parviz, you certainly know how to work your audience,' the counsel replied, looking toward the jury.

Shortly afterwards the defence and prosecution gave their summing-up speeches and the trial came to a halt. The judge summed up and instructed the jury they were not to be influenced by appearances. Their verdict must be based on the evidence only and their decision must be considered without the shadow of doubt. The jury retired to make its decision.

As Patti walked down the steps of the Supreme Court, she caught sight of the back of a short, stocky man wearing a distinctive black and purple check leather jacket walking in front of her. She hurried to catch up with him to see his face but he had disappeared, lost in the crowd.

The jury was out for three days. As the days stretched on, and constantly sick to her stomach, Patti gradually succumbed to the fear that the delay was a bad sign. Rashid's good looks, charm and adopted vulnerability had proved very persuasive to the spectators in the courtroom and quite likely to the jurors. She tried to ignore the growing dread that Rashid could escape conviction for the brutal murder of her only daughter and her mind screamed in denial of this possible travesty.

Patti and her friend, Maggie, were staying at an hotel quite close to the Supreme Court so she would be close at hand for when the jury reached its verdict. On the fourth day the prosecutor's assistant called her to advise her to get back to the court immediately as the jury were returning. She and Maggie raced to the court and burst in to the courtroom just in time for the presiding judge's associate to ask the foreman if they had reached a verdict.

The foreman was a slim young man with reddish hair and a sensitive aquiline face who was obviously nervous and trying to remain in control of his emotions.

'We have, your Honour,' he said, his voice slightly croaking and staring resolutely at the judge.

'How do you find the defendant?' the judge's associate asked.

There was a slight pause before the foreman replied, 'Not guilty,' and hung his head.

Rashid jumped to his feet and screamed, 'Allahu Akbar! Thank you Allah!'

The spectators' voices rose to a crescendo, some shouting their approval and many others in disapproval. Patti's heart sank; she had to support herself on a nearby chair to save herself from collapsing to the floor.

Dear God, no,' she thought, this can't be happening.

Chapter 14

Outside the court, Rashid was mobbed by reporters and press photographers as he smiled in jubilation at his victory.

'I very happy that justice has been done,' he announced to the press. 'I not believe I could be arrested for such a terrible crime. I want to go to my wife's grave and pray. I will help police find guilty person if they will let me. But I do not think they consider me anything more than a worthless stranger and – how you say, a nuisance and a foreigner here. It is very sad.'

Photographers' cameras flashed and television cameras followed him as he made his way, waving, to a waiting car.

But Rashid's elation was not to last. Four hours later he was re-arrested by Immigration Department officers as an illegal immigrant whilst giving a television interview at a friend's house in Chermside, where he was blatantly attempting to get publicity and financial gain from the notoriety he had received from the trial. It appeared he had not declared his first marriage on his signed visa when he entered Australia and this was an offence. He was charged with being an illegal immigrant and detained in custody.

'It doesn't matter if I am a Persian or Australian or stateless, I am still a person,' he argued, 'a human being. I have suffered enough. I have spent 375 days in jail for a crime I did not commit. I want to be treated like everyone else.'

A month later, now aged 26, a District Court ordered him to be deported from Australia.

But Allah or fate protected him once again when neither Iran, Egypt, nor Cyprus would accept him. He was released on bail awaiting deportation and moved in with an Iranian friend.

But Patti and the police weren't finished with Rashid yet. The police worked tirelessly re-examining evidence, re-interviewing witnesses and looking for new angles to bring him to some form of justice. It eventually paid off and although they were assured by their legal team that because of the double jeopardy clause in the law he could not be charged again with murder, they persisted.

Six months later, while the Palestinian Liberation Organisation were organising a deposition to Tunisia where Yasser Arafat was considering accepting him, Rashid was again arrested and charged with three counts of perjury for lying to the court in the first trial and one count of conspiracy to pervert the course of justice and this time they had the proof. Patti was elated seeing another opportunity for justice to prevail – or was it revenge? Rashid was furious and swore to beat the charges and to get rid of his vindictive mother-in-law forever.

Rashid was sent back to Boggo Road Jail on remand awaiting a bail hearing and Patti and Dennis returned to Crow's Nest to recuperate from the strain and to prepare for the upcoming trial. They were watching the late news on television when at midnight there was a loud knocking on the front door. The night was silent and dark with no street lights or any ambient light from the moon which had disappeared behind cloud. A visitor at this time of night was very unusual in such a quiet little village and Patti was immediately on guard as she peered through the front window and switched on the porch light.

A tall, attractive young woman with long blonde hair down to her shoulders and wearing a hip-length beige coat over her blue denim jeans stood at the front door. She stood with her right hand in the large pocket of her coat. Behind the woman Patti could see a white older-model car with the doors open and headlights on. Patti slid open the kitchen window slightly. There didn't appear to be any passengers in the car but Patti thought she saw two men standing in the shadows behind the vehicle.

'Yes, can I help you?' she asked nervously.

'I hope so,' the woman replied pleasantly. 'I seem to have lost my way. Could you come out here and give me directions back to the highway?'

'I'm sorry, we don't open the door to anyone at this time of night,' Patti replied. 'You'll have to turn around and head back the way you came.'

'Oh, don't be silly,' the woman said. 'It's easier to talk out here. Er, what's your name?'

Still suspicious, Patti quickly thought of a false name. 'Valerie Arnold', she said, 'From New Zealand. We've only just moved in so if you don't mind…' she began to slide the window shut.

'But surely you can help a lonely stranger find her way out of town,' the woman interrupted. 'If you'll just come out here and point in the general direction…'

'No,' Patti replied categorically. 'There's a police station just back down the road a bit near the shops. There'll be someone on duty so you can ask them.'

'Well, that's a bit stupid,' said the woman obviously becoming aggravated, 'and not very friendly or helpful. I don't really want to bother the police at this time of night. Just come out here for a minute so we can talk about it.'

'No!' said Patti, also becoming more agitated. 'Now please leave my property.'

'You silly old cow,' the woman snarled, 'there's no need to get your tits in a tangle. I just want…'

'Dennis,' Patti called out, 'get the rifle and call the police. There's a total stranger abusing me out here.'

'Bitch,' the woman muttered as she turned and fled towards the parked car catching the hem of her jeans on the barbed wire fence that Patti had installed for security. Two men appeared from the shadows and jumped into the car with the mystery woman and slammed the doors shut. The car took off at speed.

A few minutes later in response to Dennis's call, the local police constable arrived and when Patti told him what had happened and given him a description of the woman and the car, he took off in pursuit. Patti and Dennis switched on all the lights and checked the doors and windows were secure and nervously returned to the living room. There'd be no sleep that night.

Sometime later there was another knock at the door and the police constable called out, 'It's all right, Mrs Price, its Constable Wright.'

The constable told them he'd caught up with the car and given chase but it had sped up to over 150 kilometres an hour and disappeared into the night. He'd followed for over fifty kilometres but they evaded him. Although the vehicle was an old model it had obviously been hotted up and adapted for high speed.

'But surely you got the number plate,' Dennis said.

The constable shook his head in embarrassment. 'It'd been muddied up,' said the constable, 'impossible to read.'

'What d'you reckon?' Dennis said to Patti after the officer had left after assuring them they'd keep an eye on the place.

'Isn't it obvious?' Patti replied. 'They were after me. Rashid's up for parole tomorrow and having me as a hostage or killed would help him make bail, wouldn't it?'

'I think you're being a bit paranoid,' Dennis said. 'Killing you would make it even more suspicious, don't you think?' he said wryly.

'He wants me dead, Dennis. I know he murdered Tianne. If only they'd put me on the witness stand.'

'I don't think they need your evidence this time, Patti, I think they've got enough to put him away for a long time.'

'Oh, God, I hope so. This is driving me crazy.'

Dennis put his arms around her shoulders and tried to comfort her but Patti's fear remained.

Patti and Detective Sergeant Porter waited in the foyer of the Supreme Court.

'They've set the bail at ten thousand dollars,' Porter smirked. 'There's no way the bastard will raise that much.'

But within minutes, Rashid, smiling and again dressed and groomed to perfection, arrived in the foyer accompanied by a large, unsavoury-looking man.

'Oh, Jesus,' Porter said, eyeing the couple.

'What?' said Patti, following his gaze.

'The old bastard with our friend,' Porter snarled, 'that's Joshua Jamieson, underworld crime boss. Three guesses where Rashid got his bail. I wonder what he's promised to do in return.'

Rashid looked directly at Patti and roared with laughter.

Chapter 15

Patti received a telephone call from a man identifying himself as Andrew Middleton from Counter Intelligence asking if she could spare the time for a short interview. Patti was surprised to be receiving such a request but agreed. Middleton sent a car for her and she was taken to a small, sterile office at the Toowoomba police station.

The Insignificant Man smiled and greeted her charmingly confirming he was Andrew Middleton from Counter Intelligence with a plain Public Service business card giving his name and a private telephone number. He directed her to a chair at the only desk in the room and sat opposite her.

'Thank you for coming, Mrs Price. This is only a routine interview to see if you have any information that may be of interest to us in a minor ongoing investigation.'

'I take it this has to do with Rashid El Parviz and the recent abortive trial,' she said, suspecting this could be the only reason for such an interview at this particular time.

Middleton smiled benignly. 'Yes, I'm so sorry for your loss and the outcome of the trial,' he said, genuinely.

'Thank you,' Patti replied. 'It was a travesty.'

'Yes, legal outcomes don't always work out as expected,' he agreed, 'and this must be very painful for you but as El Parviz is of foreign citizenship we have to investigate his background to see if there are any inconsistencies or legalities that may be of interest to us and the safety of the country.' He paused to draw a pad across the desk and picked up a beautiful black and gold fountain pen. 'Now, what exactly do you know about Rashid El Parviz?'

'Very little,' Patti replied. 'I know he claims to be an Iranian, or Persian, as he prefers to be known,' she said disdainfully. 'I met him in Cyprus – Limassol, actually, with Tianne. He said he was the manager of a nightclub in Larnaca but I suspect he was only a waiter. I only ever met him a couple of times but Tianne told me he used to beat her and treat her appallingly. I begged her to leave him but she was besotted with him. I know he killed her.'

'But what about his background?' Middleton pressed. 'Surely Tianne told you more about him?'

'No, she was a very private person and wouldn't discuss his background. I don't think she knew much either. He was a Muslim and didn't think women had the right to know their husband's business affairs. I know they travelled a lot overseas – Germany, France, Greece, London, Egypt and the Middle East. I don't know what they were doing there, just tourists I suppose.'

'And there's nothing else you can tell me?'

'Only that he was a professional charmer with a narcissist complex and a monster,' she said with loathing. 'And of course, he only used my daughter to get into this country on her passport because he didn't have one of his own,'

'And why do you think she did that?'

'She loved him and wanted to help him. Tianne was like that; she'd do anything for him. She was a very strong, loyal and independent character as a rule but he was her weakness.' Patti thought for a moment and said, 'She once told me he'd admitted killing people when he was in the army over in Lebanon.' She thought for a moment. 'Maybe he was an agent.'

Middleton made a note on the pad.

'She did tell me she knew other things about him but she never elaborated.'

'Pity,' Middleton said.

'To be frank, Mr Middleton, I'm scared. I know what he's capable of and if he thinks I might know anything that may be a danger to him, he's quite likely to come after me too. I think I would like a gun, a revolver to protect myself if needed. Is there any way you can help me with that?'

Middleton looked at her speculatively for a long moment. 'I don't think that will be necessary, Mrs. Price. We'll be keeping an eye on you and him I can assure you. Perhaps you may think of wearing some sort of disguise – a wig maybe?'

Patti almost laughed. 'And a moustache, maybe?' she scoffed. 'I don't think that would save me, Mr Middleton. I've already had a scare from one of his friends who tried to get me outside the house one night.'

'Perhaps if you improved the security around your house?'

'I've already installed a high fence, padlocks, alarms and some barbed wire around my house,' she said. 'I can't afford a twenty-four-hour trained bodyguard. My husband already thinks I'm paranoid.'

'I'm sure you'll be fine, Mrs Price, and as I said we'll be keeping an eye on you.'

'Why do I not feel reassured?' Patti replied.

The Insignificant Man smiled.

Chapter 16

In the courtroom, the charges were read out.

'Rashid El Parviz. You have been charged with three counts of perjury: one, that you falsely swore you did not kill your wife Tianne Allen-Kelly on the eleventh of October 1988; two, that you falsely swore that you had never hit anyone; and three, that you falsely swore that you did not know a fellow prison inmate, Michael J Carter at the time of your previous trial. You are also charged with conspiracy to prevent the course of justice relating to that trial.'

Rashid was asked if he pleaded guilty or not guilty.

'Not guilty,' Rashid called out loudly, this time clutching a Bible in his hand. He obviously felt he had to play all the angles.

The prosecution, again led by Joseph Delaney, opened the case for the prosecution re-stating that they would prove Rashid had committed perjury when he lied to the jury giving testimony that he did not kill his wife, that he did in fact strike his wife several times during the course of their short but stormy relationship, and that he had spoken to and admitted to Michael Carter that he had killed his wife and had asked him for an alibi. And the prosecution will also prove that the charge of perverting the course of justice was committed when the accused bribed two fellow inmates, Steve Collins and Trevor Manders, to supply him with an alibi for the night of the murder.

Steve Collins, one of the conspirators, was called to the witness stand.

'Mr Collins, do you now confess to lying to the court when you gave evidence in the previous trial stating that you and your friend, Trevor Manders, provided the accused with an alibi by stating you spent the night of the eleventh of October, 1988, together at Rashid Parviz's residence at Paddington?'

'I do,' Collins replied.

'So you now confess this was in fact a falsehood and you did not spend the night in the accused's company?'

'That is correct.'

'And why did you invent that story, Mr Collins?'

'To give him an alibi for his wife's murder and I wanted to get back at the cops.'

'You mean to discredit Homicide Detective Sergeant Porter, is that correct?'

'Yes sir, we found out Carter had told Porter about his chat with Rashid. Rashid was furious and said we'd work around it and blame Porter for lying about it.'

'And did the accused request you to make that false statement, Mr Collins?'

'He did and he laughed and said we'd really stick it up the prosecution and the cops.'

'And why have you now confessed to that crime, Mr Collins?'

'I'd had enough. I wanted to set things right. I didn't want to defend a murderer.'

'And were you threatened or did you conspire with the police or the Director of Prosecutions to accept any bribe or compensation to make this statement?'

'No, I wasn't, and did not receive compensation. I just wanted to do the right thing.'

'Very commendable of you, Mr Collins,' Delaney said drily. 'That is all, thank you.'

Rashid muttered under his breath and glared at Collins.

The cross examination of the second witness, Collins' accomplice, Trevor Manders, followed the same pattern but he claimed he was sick of living in a world of lies and 'falseness' and wanted to make a fresh start. He also revealed that Michael Carter, looking for personal advantage, had reported the planned alibi to Detective Sergeant Porter. Rashid found out and was furious and conspired with Collins and Manders to bring Carter down and discredit Detective Sergeant Porter to whom Carter had supposedly reported Rashid's confession.

What was not revealed was that both Collins and Manders, although separated in Boggo Road Jail, had conspired together and succeeded in escaping prison with knotted sheets and a prison-made grappling hook and had been recaptured at Coolangatta airport with a stash of heroin. They had agreed to change their original evidence regarding the alibi they'd given in the murder trial in return for a lesser sentence.

Michael Carter was then called to the witness stand.

'Mr Carter,' Delaney asked, 'will you please state the conversation you had with the accused in the holding pen at Boggo Road Jail regarding the murder of the accused's bigamous wife, Tianne Allen-Price?'

'Yeah, I killed the bitch, he said, but he said he needed an alibi to beat the rap.'

'And did you agree to give him an alibi, Mr Carter?'

'No. I advised him to plead guilty and admit to manslaughter.'

'Did he offer you any recompense for an alibi, Mr Carter?'

'Yeah, he said he could get me some heroin smuggled in.'

'And you declined the offer?'

'I certainly did. But I heard he'd got a couple of other lags to do it for him.'

'Objection,' cried the defence.

Under cross examination by the defence, Carter admitted to the counsel that he had offered to give evidence for the prosecution in other cases including murder and drug trials in return for a full pardon, a new identity, a $50,000 reward for information on another murder, a guarantee from the Police Commissioner that no further charges would be brought against him in the future and that he be released into police protection.

'But that offer had been rejected, is that not true, Mr Carter?' replied the prosecution.

'Yes sir,' said Michael Carter.

The jury were transported to Boggo Road Jail to view the holding pen where it was claimed Rashid had held the conversation with Michael Carter.

Leslie Buckley, a prison officer who worked in the Boggo Road infirmary, gave evidence that he had several times witnessed Collins and Manders in quiet conversation with Rashid while he was being observed for possible hepatitis.

On a roll, Delaney then called Detective Inspector Shaw from the Cairns police station.

Shaw gave evidence that Rashid had been arrested on a domestic violence charge in Cairns and that his wife, Tianne, had been admitted to hospital with significant wounds to her face and arms but her husband, Rashid Parviz had been let off on a twelve-month good-behaviour bond.

'Objection,' called the defence, 'irrelevant to this case.'

'Demonstrating the accused's previous behaviour of violence towards his wife, Your Honour,' replied the prosecution.

'Overruled,' the judge replied to the defence.

This had caused a stir in the courtroom as did the following evidence from a Chief Inspector Bowen, who had been brought out from Scotland Yard in London to testify that Rashid Parviz had been arrested and charged for domestic violence in The Old Bailey for causing bodily harm to his wife,

Tianne Parviz, in 1987, and was subsequently sentenced to three months' imprisonment. Again his wife had been hospitalised with significant wounds to the head and body.

Over the next few weeks many witnesses came forward to repeat or refute the evidence they had given in the first trial including a young woman, Claudette Young, a former friend of Rashid's, who had testified in favour of Rashid saying that she had felt very sorry for him. She said he appeared to be distraught with his marriage and seemed to be on the verge of a nervous breakdown and she had suggested that he leave Tianne and return to his first wife and children. On further meetings with him he had talked about killing his wife as the only way of getting her out of his life.

It also seemed that the priest who had given a favourable character reference for Rashid in the murder trial had also changed his mind when Rashid had asked to receive instructions in becoming a Catholic to influence the jury in his favour for the second trial.

Patti was thrilled with this evidence but was also appalled it and other incriminating evidence had not been allowed to be submitted in the initial trial. The prosecution had a lot to answer for, she believed, and she was also suspicious that unseen forces had been at work to free Rashid but for what purpose she had no idea.

But the way of the Law is confusing to the lay person as to what the Law sees as admissible and what is prejudicial to the accused. A very fine line is drawn to bring about truth and justice and sometimes that line is crossed.

Chapter 17

Patti was discussing the implications with Porter during an intermission in the trial when she noticed a very smartly dressed elderly woman standing nearby staring at her. She was certain that she had seen this woman following her several times since the trial had begun and became a little anxious. When she excused herself from Porter to visit the ladies' room, the woman followed her in.

'Do you mind if I talk to you?' the woman asked when they were alone.

The woman didn't appear threatening but being a little paranoid from the strain she had been through over the last months, Patti wandered over and stood close to the door in case she needed to escape quickly. 'Yes, of course,' she said.

'Thank you,' the woman said in obvious relief. 'I had to talk to you. You see, I'm the mother of the man who was foreman of the jury at the first trial.'

Her name was Clarke and she wanted desperately to vindicate her son's behaviour in the first trial. Patti was intrigued. At last she may get answers as to why Rashid had been exonerated.

'You see,' Mrs Clarke explained, 'at the first count there were about five members of the jury who voted guilty, three not guilty and four undecided. My son, James, didn't agree with the verdict but was forced to go along with some of the others because he was inexperienced with the rules of the law as were most of the other jurors. The only instruction the judge gave them was their decision had to be reached without a reasonable shadow of doubt. But how do you measure reasonable doubt?' Mrs Clarke said. 'What level of reasonable is reasonable?

'And there was doubt in their minds, you see. Apparently there was one man who said right from the beginning he had no doubt in his mind that the accused was not guilty as there was no hard evidence and he would never change his mind and he didn't, no matter what the other jurors said. And there was another young man who was the son of the owner of a string of those "adult" pornography shops in Tweed Heads whose father had been murdered in 1986, who was also adamant that Rashid was innocent.

'But then one of the most compelling arguments came about over the mention of the Jeffrey Maddox case which you may remember had become big news during the Fitzgerald inquiry the year before when Maddox had been found guilty of his father's murder and supposedly confessed. But it turned out under investigation he'd been put under extreme pressure and the police had threatened him with bringing his family in as accessories if he didn't confess. So Maddox had been forced to give a written confession against his will for the murder.

'So you see the Maddox case kept coming up and with that in their minds the jurors suspected that any evidence the police gave was therefore not to be trusted.

'The jury argued back and forth for three days and they were still uncertain.

'Eventually,' Mrs Clarke continued, 'because they were bending over to give the benefit of the doubt, the vote was ten not guilty and two, including James, guilty.

'What else could he do?' Mrs Clarke wailed. 'He argued for the guilty plea but if you changed your vote you had to justify your new decision and make sure the others agreed. The judge had also told them if there was any doubt it had to be taken into account. Yes, they eventually found him not guilty but by the end vote if they'd been allowed a majority vote the verdict might have been different.

'James always believed it was the wrong decision,' she said tearfully, 'and he has suffered dreadfully ever since. He has the most terrible nightmares, he's been so ill he hasn't been able to work, he's lost so much weight he looks like a skeleton.' She paused and looked into Patti's eyes. 'I'm afraid he'll go insane or try to kill himself. He needs forgiveness, your forgiveness. Please.'

Patti couldn't help but be moved by this poor mother's plea. She suddenly realised what some jurors go through when they're chosen to sit in judgement of another human being with very little option, legal knowledge or instruction. There is always so much information ruled not admissible. It's not always what's said but what is left unsaid in a trial that can lead to a dismissal or a conviction

They cannot feel the pain and suffering of the victim, they can really have no idea what the families and loved ones of the victim go through. They are usually simple people who can't always be blamed for the unintentional wrong they do.

Maybe a majority decision would be fairer, Patti thought.

'Of course I forgive him, Mrs Clarke,' she said, placing a conciliatory hand on the mother's arm. 'Please assure him of that. Maybe we'll get him this time.'

Chapter 18

On her return to the courtroom foyer, Patti noticed a face she recognised. The man waved to her and made his way across to speak to her. Patti recognised him as Louis Romano, a rather shady nightclub owner she had occasionally worked for.

'Hi Patti,' he said, laughing and enfolding her in his massive arms. 'What ya doin' here, kiddo?'

'Trying to get a monster convicted of murdering my daughter, Louis,' she said.

'Oh.' He looked saddened. 'Sorry to hear that Patti, and how's it goin'? he asked holding her at arm's length.

'Well, I don't know, Louis, he beat the charge the first time so I'm not holding my breath – well, I am actually,' she said smiling and contradicting herself.

'He was tried before?' Louis asked. 'I been outta town in Calabria for health reasons. I didn't hear. What happened?'

'He was found not guilty despite all the evidence.'

'Hey, Double Jeopardy, kiddo, you can't get him again.' He leaned forward and whispered in her ear, 'You shoulda called me.'

Double Jeopardy, where you couldn't be tried for the same crime twice if you were acquitted at the first trial, was in force at that time.

'Now I wish I had, Louis,' she replied. 'If anyone deserves to be shot it's him. At best he deserves to be locked up and the key thrown away. We're going for three counts of perjury and one of perverting the course of justice this time and the evidence is pretty good.'

'You got my number if he gets off again,' he said winking at her.

A policeman in uniform walked by and Louis quickly excused himself and left.

Chapter 19

At last Rashid was again called to the witness stand for a marathon battle between the prosecutor, defence and the accused, which dragged on for many exhausting days. Rashid continued to deny lying to the court, often asking for questions to be repeated and explained more clearly and often replying that he 'no understand'. His accent thickened and at times his replies were purposely difficult to understand. He continued to vehemently deny that he had murdered Tianne or that he had physically assaulted her claiming he only protected himself from her attacks. He accused witnesses for the prosecution of lying and particularly the police whose evidence was at best questionable given the current public opinion held since the Fitzgerald Crime and Corruption Inquiry. But throughout the proceedings he maintained his attractive suave appearance and charm and consistently appealed directly to the jury, much to the chagrin of the judge.

After an exhaustive month-long trial, the prosecution, defence and finally the judge gave their summing up and the jury retired to make its decision.

Patti, Dennis and Maggie retired to a nearby café but nobody felt like eating so they settled for several cups of coffee. Maggie and Dennis were very upbeat but Patti still had doubts about the outcome.

'He's such a clever bastard,' she said. 'We've been here before. I wouldn't put anything past him. It seems to me that this is another murder trial rather than perjury. And if that turns out to be the case, he'll appeal and invoke the Double Jeopardy ruling. We have been warned about that by the Public Prosecutor.'

'If he's found guilty of perjury he'll still do time,' Dennis said. 'At least that will be something.'

'But not enough,' Patti said fiercely. 'I want him to go down for murder. He killed our daughter, Dennis, lying to the court isn't the same. He's got to be seen for what he is, a vicious, cold-blooded murderer.'

'Oh, Patti,' Maggie said, putting her hand on Patti's shoulder, 'you're a trouper remember, keep your chin up. The show isn't over until the fat lady sings, right? I think we should go back and get some rest. It'll probably be a few days before we get the verdict so I think we need to keep our strength up.'

The fat lady didn't stop singing for three days but when she did she finished on a high note.

Rashid lowered his head as the jury returned to the courtroom with their verdict.

'And how do you find the defendant on the charge of Conspiring to Pervert the Course of Justice,' asked the judge's associate, 'guilty or not guilty?'

'Not guilty,' replied the foreman of the jury.

There was an audible gasp from the spectators and Patti's heart sank in despondency. 'Not again, please not again,' she whispered to God.

'And how do you find the defendant on the charges of perjury for lying to the court on the charges of murdering his wife and lying in regard to assaulting his wife?'

'Guilty as charged,' came the reply.

'And what is your verdict in relationship to the defendant lying as to having admitted his guilt to Michael Carter – guilty or not guilty?'

There was a pause as the foremen looked directly at Rashid. 'Guilty as charged on all three charges,' said the foreman.

The court erupted and Patti's heart leapt in joy as tears of relief flooded her eyes. Patti and Dennis embraced; their long arduous battle at last partly justified. Emotionless, Rashid stared straight ahead giving little outward reaction to the verdict.

The court was brought to order and Rashid was commanded to stand for the judge's statement and sentence. Queensland's legal history was about to be rewritten. This was the first time anyone acquitted of murder had then been brought back to court on perjury charges and found guilty.

Rashid declined to make any statement on his own behalf.

The judge was scathing of Rashid, claiming he had gone a long way in procuring his acquittal and had grossly taken advantage of the current distrust of the police. He also stated that Rashid had used his considerable charm to his advantage with the jury of the first trial and that clear inference had been drawn that he did in fact murder his wife in a premeditated and utterly ruthless fashion.

'What you have done has struck at the very heart of the judicial process,' he declared. He then sentenced Rashid to the maximum allowed fourteen years' imprisonment for perjury.

A smiling and elated Patti and Dennis, together with the defence and prosecution counsels, were mobbed outside the court by newspaper and television cameras and reporters for their reaction to the verdict.

'I knew he had perjured himself during the murder trial and I knew we could prove it,' Patti said. 'Everyone said we were wasting our time and money but I couldn't give up and let him get away with killing Tianne. For her sake, we had to keep going. Fourteen years isn't enough under the circumstances but at least he will no longer be walking the streets a free man, free to kill again.'

In a later interview Patti told a journalist, 'At first the office of Queensland's Attorney General refused to help in bringing Rashid to trial for perjury suggesting we had no chance at all in gaining a conviction.'

But when the Labor Party swept into power in 1989 Patti had tried again. The newly appointed Attorney General reviewed the case and Rashid was re-arrested on the four charges of conspiracy and perjury.

Patti had worked closely with the new Crown prosecutor and Gold Coast police throughout the case and knowing Rashid's over-confident conman tricks, had tried a few of her own tactics to unnerve him during the trial.

'It was really a battle of wits,' Patti had said. 'I was well aware of the danger of underestimating him. I always made sure I would wear something of Tianne's to help unnerve him at the trial and I didn't miss a moment in case I picked up something he let slip.

'I was so determined to nail my daughter's killer I would've done anything. I even tried to buy a gun to kill him if I couldn't manage to get justice through legal means. It would've been worth it. They wouldn't give me a licence,' she said sadly.

'My daughter had been infatuated with Rashid but before she was killed, she no longer loved him. She was simply terrified of him. She said he would never let her go and he didn't.

'Tianne died the most horrific death and she must've been absolutely terrified during those final hours of her life,' Patti said, with tears welling in her eyes. 'The brutality of it has been the most difficult to accept.

'He is a highly intelligent, cold and calculating, manipulative murderer and should never be released,' she said vehemently.

'The jury's decision in the perjury trial made legal history,' Patti said, 'why not make another first and have a retrial on the original charge of murder? The judge gave Rashid the maximum sentence he could for perjury, but that really isn't enough under the circumstances. Tianne just didn't know what she was dealing with when she tangled with Rashid El Parviz.'

Patti visited her daughter's grave in the cemetery across the road from the modest, rambling old timber farmhouse Patti and Dennis called home. She placed a bunch of beautiful spring flowers in a vase next to the headstone.

After a short prayer, she whispered, 'Rest peacefully now, my darling. We got him. At last we got him.'

Chapter 20

But the saga wasn't to end there. As Patti had feared, an appeal was lodged by the defence counsel and was heard several weeks later. Patti had not been officially informed of the appeal but attended the Supreme Court for the subsequent hearing. Six crimson-robed adjudicators sat in judgement. Patti was informed later that after the hearing one of the judges said to the counsel for the Public Prosecution, 'If the evidence in the perjury trial had been presented in the initial murder trial, we wouldn't be here now.'

However, the appeal was upheld on the grounds that the trial was actually a murder trial and therefore the Double Jeopardy ruling of a defendant not being allowed to be tried for the same offence after a jury acquittal, came into effect, and the first two charges of perjury, that he falsely swore that he did not kill his wife and that he falsely swore he did not hit anyone were dismissed on legal technicalities. One charge of perjury: that he did not know and had never met one of the witnesses in the murder trial, Michael Carter, remained for future possible prosecution and a trial date was to be set.

As he left the High Court, Rashid paused directly in front of Patti, looked directly into her face and laughed. He was released and walked free.

Although deeply disappointed at the finding, Patti was not totally surprised as she had been warned of the likelihood of the outcome by the police and the Director of Prosecutions. Such were the vagaries of the legal system and an inept defence which allowed a brutal murderer to escape natural justice.

Several months later Patti received a letter from the Director of Prosecutions stating,

'I refer to the outstanding case of perjury against Rashid El Parviz and am instructed by the Director to write personally to advise you that the Director has decided to proceed no further in the prosecution of the abovenamed in respect of one count of falsely swearing at his murder trial that he did not know and had not met, a man called Carter.

> *As you will be only too painfully aware, this unfortunate matter has dragged on for a considerable length of time, and the Director has now taken the view that it is **not in the public interest** for Mr Rashid El Parviz to stand trial on this remaining count.*

There was no doubt the strain of Tianne's murder and the ensuing two-year battle for justice had taken its toll on Patti and Dennis's marriage. Patti understandably had become completely absorbed in the case and had suffered many disappointments and hardships along the way. Dennis had tried to be supportive but found himself being pushed further apart from his wife as she tried to cope with the constant strain. There had been many episodes of illness and Patti was so distraught, she could no longer work. Although communication between the two became difficult they remained married and still continued to work together.

Patti and Dennis sold their house in Crow's Nest and moved to a new home, hopefully free of memories, in outer Brisbane. But no matter the change in location, memories are packed away in the cardboard boxes of our minds and stored away forever.

Chapter 21

Four young Sunni Muslim men sat at their usual table in the Marqaha coffee house in Albion. Marqaha was an Islamic term for the euphoria produced when drinking coffee. They were all dressed in jeans and T-shirts: Abdul-Aleem, which meant 'servant of the most high', Imaad, which meant 'pillar of faith', Jaafar, 'glory of the faith' and Khaldoon, 'eternal', were in their early twenties and were involved in intense, whispered conversation.

'He has brought our group into disrepute,' said Jaafar, 'we don't need that. We have enough trouble with the police as it is.'

'Remember he was the founder of our group,' said Khaldoon. 'We must respect and protect him.'

'But he has a responsibility to us as well,' said Imaad. 'He is supposed to protect us and his trial has brought unwanted negative publicity to our cause. I think he should be exiled and barred from any further demonstrations or involvement.'

'But he is so good at arranging demonstrations,' said Khaldoon. 'He can charm the nijab from any of the female protestors. '

'And the men will follow him anywhere,' Abdul-Aleem said.

'But we do not want our leader to be suspected of cold-blooded murder,' Imaad said. 'It will destroy our image.'

Jafaar laughed. 'What image? We are looked upon as radicals by most of the people in the street. We don't have an image to protect.'

'We know the road is long,' Khaldoon said, 'but the struggle must continue until the minds of the infidel are freed of suspicion and mistrust. Besides, he was acquitted.'

'And then arrested again four hours later,' Jafaar said. 'There is every chance he will be deported for being an illegal. The problem will be solved. '

'If anybody will take him,' said Imaad. 'They can't just send him off back to Cyprus or Egypt without their approval.'

'Maybe Yasser Arafat will take him back,' said Khaldoon. 'They were very close in Lebanon. I heard the PLO has sent a delegation to Tunisia with a request.'

'Arafat has to look to his image as well now he is making overtures to America and the West for acceptance,' said Jafaar. 'It mightn't look good for him either if he harbour's a suspected wife-murderer.'

'But he was acquitted,' repeated Khaldoon.

The other three all looked at him with various levels of scepticism.

Abs, wearing his black and purple leather jacket entered, nodded and joined them at the table.

'Allahu Akbar,' Abs said as he sat down, completely unaware of the tiny microphone taped under the table. Ghassan, the Shiite barrister whose parents and three-year-old sister had been killed in a suicide bombing in Damascus in 2004 by Sunni militants, disappeared into the back room to adjust the volume of the pick up on the microphone receiver.

Chapter 22

The Insignificant Man was at the airport to see Rashid off to Sydney. He still had not been granted a passport as he was still considered an illegal immigrant and now a possible terrorist threat. He would always be tracked and on the Terrorist Radar List. The agent wandered over to Rashid and stood in front of him.

'Now Rashid,' he said quietly, 'you may have got away with murder with a little help from ex-friends but I warn you, any hint of you misbehaving for the rest of your life will have dire consequences. It just so happens we have in our possession Tianne's fingernail clippings with the residue of your skin still on them. That would be considered "fresh evidence" and allow another murder charge to be laid and you wouldn't beat that one. So you will just disappear and stay out of the limelight for the rest of your life, won't you, there's a good boy.'

He turned to go, stopped and turned back.

'Oh, and by the way, you might consider getting a job, if you can, in a factory or as a cleaner because you certainly won't be getting any more glamorous trips around the world as a double agent, or even a single agent if it comes to that. The PLO has become respectable so they won't touch you and neither will any other country. Your wife in Cyprus has divorced you and you'll never see her or your sons again, or your parents because they've disowned you. You're on your own, son.'

Rashid just stared at him as inscrutably as the agent stared at him.

'That's all right,' he said, 'I'm used to working on my own.'

Once more the dazzling, confident smile then he turned and walked through the departure gates to the waiting aircraft.

Acknowledgements

My thanks to ex-magistrate James Barbeler for his legal expertise, to Julia Carroll for her support and encouragement, and to Patti for giving me free access to her records, memories and her life, for her amazing story.

Bryon Williams

I feel a great debt of gratitude to Queensland. When I came here as a young teenager I found new and lasting friends, a long career in the Industry, and learnt much from the many wonderful artists I met through Theatre Royal Queensland.

Finally, heartfelt thanks to Bryon Williams without whom this book could not have been written.

Patti Allen-Price

www.ingramcontent.com/pod-product-compliance
Lightning Source LLC
Chambersburg PA
CBHW072047290426
44110CB00014B/1588